Marketing in the Building Industry

ISBN 1-59113-057-3

Published 2001

Published by Butcher Consulting Group, LTD, 3687 Concord Road, York, PA, 17402, U.S.A.

Manufactured in the United States of America.

Booklocker.com, Inc.
2001

Marketing in the Building Industry

Scott D. Butcher

Marketing in the Building Industry

To Marla and Don Butcher, who
never told their son that
he *couldn't* do something—instilling
in him the value that there is
nothing he can't do!

Table of Contents

Introduction

A lot can change in ten years. In fact, anymore it seems that a lot can change in one year or two years.

Ten years is the amount of time I've been involved with marketing in the design and construction industries. *Marketing in the Building Industry* includes several articles written over an eight-year period, from 1993 to 2001. As I compiled this book, I read many of these articles for the first time in several years. And, man, how things have changed.

The first marketing article I ever had published, "Structuring for Business Development," was written before I knew much about the Internet. In fact, it was written before *most* of us knew much about the Internet. How did we live without it? Now, nary a day goes by when I don't surf the 'Net.

Computers have totally changed the way we do business, and they continue to do so. We've gone from using markers and easels for presentations to Palm Pilots hooked into three-pound, high-resolution computer projectors.

But what has really changed? Are things really *that* different?

Actually, no. We still need to target quality prospects, promote our capabilities, differentiate ourselves from the competition, and deliver a competent solution at a fair price within a reasonable schedule.

Technology may change. Our marketing tools may change. But the end result hasn't changed—and won't be changing anytime soon. With that in mind, I'm pleased to share *Marketing in the Building Industry*, because good marketing never goes out of style!

— Scott D. Butcher, CPSM

Marketing Planning for Professional Services Firms

I have to be really lost to stop and ask for directions. I mean *really* lost. I can't say I'm a great user of maps, either. This probably explains why I usually have to leave extra early to ensure arrival at my destination on time. I remember one trip to Baltimore when I drove right by my final destination, but I was stuck on the expressway and the closest off-ramp was almost two miles away and, of course, I didn't have a map with me. Hey—I knew *about* where the place was. I knew I *wanted* to get there. I just didn't have any directions, which at the time I figured wasn't a bad thing. Well, two hours after I first drove within one hundred yards of my destination (on a limited access highway!), I finally stopped, swallowed my pride (or is the correct word "stupidity"?), and asked for directions. Five minutes later I was there.

All that time I had a goal: to arrive at my destination. (The goal soon became to arrive at my destination safely, which you would easily understand if you were driving through the same neighborhoods I was!) I knew how to get close, just not close enough. And that is a problem with many marketing plans for professional services firms: lots of goals, no road map to get there. Of course, that's assuming that there even is a formal marketing plan in existence, which is by no means a given in our industry. I'm always amazed when I talk with colleagues whose firms, both large and small, have no formal marketing plan. Developing and implementing a marketing plan is essential for the long-term success of any company, and does not have to be a painstaking task.

First, you have to determine the purpose of the marketing plan. Why does it exist? To do that, look no further that the company's mission statement (again, assuming that a mission statement exists). The mission statement is your destination. The marketing plan, in conjunction with the strategic plan, is your road map to get there.

As a marketer, it is your responsibility to determine how to arrive at the mission statement. What roads should be taken? Which should be avoided? Where might road construction and delays be encountered? Where might there be speed traps? By looking at the Big Picture, considering all possible scenarios, you will avoid the trap of entering the Wonderful World of Myopia.

Throughout this report, we will be incorporating examples from a hypothtical firm, Designs-R-Us. Here is a quick overview of the company:

Designs-R-Us, Indiana Office

Employees: 8
Services:
- HVAC Engineering
- Electrical Engineering
- Plumbing Engineering
- Fire Protection Engineering

Client Types:
- Architects
- Local Government
- State Government
- Federal Government

Project Types:
- Correctional Facilities
- Classroom Buildings
- Dormitories
- Office Buildings
- Postal Facilities
- Assisted Living Facilities

Your firm may very well be larger and more complex than Designs-R-Us. The Designs-R-Us exhibits found throughout this report have been simplified—just enough to get you started.

Situational Analysis

The first section you should develop is the Situational Analysis, which is a discussion of the current competitive environment. Think of it as the setting in which your story unfolds. How has your firm fared over the past year? How about your competitors? Which markets were hot, and which ones were not? What trends have been witnessed? The Situational Analysis is a summary of the past year, and how that relates to the next year. It should be informative, but also brief—no more than 1500 words. Remember, you want the managers to actually *read* your Marketing Plan. Once you have completed this section, you now have a map. What you don't have yet are your directions. In the "This Year's Goals and Objectives" section you will mark up the map not only to determine where you are going, but also how you plan to get there.

Designs-R-Us, Indiana Office

SITUATIONAL ANALYSIS

This past year was a challenging one for the Indiana office of Designs-R-Us. While the company's Pennsylvania and Texas offices had very successful years, the Indiana office was unable to obtain its expansion goals. Our staff remains at eight, our revenues remain stagnant.

One reason that we did not meet our goals is related to the local economic conditions. With approximately 60% of our annual revenues coming through architectural clients, much of our success depends upon their success. Unfortunately, our single largest architectural client – Indianapolis Architectural Group – downsized their staff and got out of the collegiate market entirely. Two years ago we received almost $180,000 in fees from IAG. Last year that number dropped to $115,000, and with their refocused marketing strategy, it is entirely possible that our annual workload with IAG will drop below $100,000.

Further complicating matters was the state's decision to put the Century Project on hold. While that project is now scheduled to be released in the second quarter of this year, we had counted on it to comprise a significant amount of workload last year.

Even with these setbacks, which were both beyond our control, we were able to book enough work to maintain our current staff size. Existing clients accounted for approximately 80% of our volume, and we also were awarded a fairly significant design commission with a new client, Hancock Contractors, Inc.

In recent years, the design-build project delivery system has negatively impacted our sales and marketing effort. Contractors are providing turn-key design and construction solutions, with much of the mechanical, electrical, and plumbing engineering now handled directly by the trade contractors, not engineering firms. That stated, Hancock Contractors incorporated our firm into their team to pursue the Knightstown Post Office. The were awarded the contract, resulting in a booking of over $80,000.

> The relationship has been positive, and we are now exploring more opportunities for teaming.
>
> As we look to the coming year, the state should begin releasing funds for projects previously approved by the legislature. Not only will this have a direct impact on Designs-R-Us—in relation to the Century Project—but it will also open the door to pursue several new projects, which are now scheduled to be advertised in the third quarter.
>
> Because of the loss of revenues from IAG, we will need to proactively market to the architectural community, not only to maintain market share but to expand our share and thus our staff.

Evaluation of Last Year's Goals and Objectives

The next section you should develop is a review of the previous year's goals. Everything in a successful Marketing Plan is interrelated. This evaluation springs from the Situational Analysis and helps to form future goals. Even if your firm had no formal plan last year, chances are that you still had some goals: Obtain $5 million in sales; Secure work with Big Client X; Conduct a seminar; and so forth. If you had a formal plan, all the much better. Evaluate each individual goal, and spare no punches. If you made your goal, great. Why? Explain how your firm succeeded in achieving that particular goal. If you didn't make your goal, why not? Whose responsibility was it, and why was the goal not achieved? In many cases, you may find that you only had goals, but no strategies. Again, let us return to our map analogy. Your goal is your destination, and thus your Marketing Plan is a series of destinations. Your strategies, on the other hand, are your directions. "Go one block and turn left" is a strategy; "Stop when you reach 123 Market Street" is a goal.

After you have picked apart the successes and failures of the previous year—and again, brevity is the operative word—you are ready to begin your next section: Target Market.

Target Market

Your Target Market can be defined in several ways: Geographic, Client Type, and Building (Project) Type. Which geographic territory does your firm service? Is the world your oyster, or are you a hometown boy? Are 90% of your clients within a fifty-mile radius, or within the continental United States?

Go to the store and purchase a map (the kind created by a cartographer, not the kind you are creating!), and start to circle the locations of your projects. Once you have finished, you will have a visual representation of your existing Geographic Target Market. Are there any holes on the map? If so, does your firm want those holes to be holes? Or are they new areas that you would like to move into? If so, mark those areas for growth. Do no more than that, though. In a later section you will plot the course to achieve success in those areas.

Geographic Target Market (by Radius)

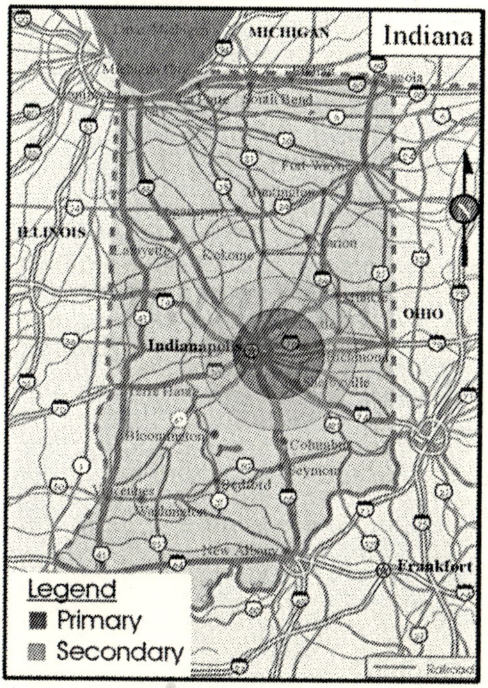

Geographic Target Market (by County)

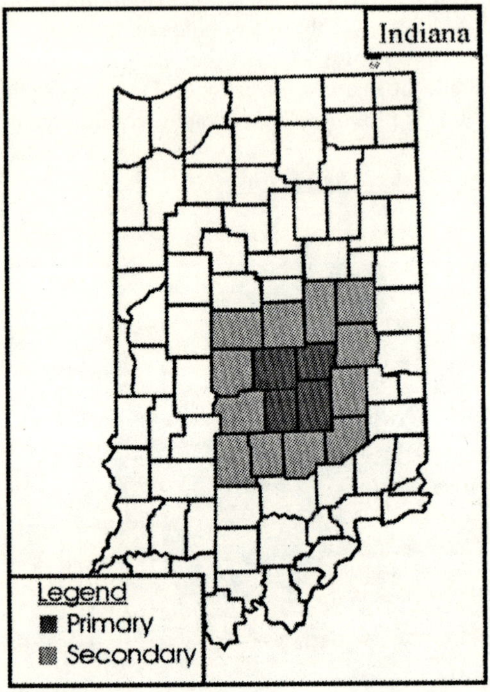

Designs-R-Us, Indiana Office

GEOGRAPHIC TARGET MARKET

1. Primary Counties
Hancock
Johnson
Marion
Shelby

2. Secondary Counties
Bartholomew
Boone
Brown
Delaware
Decatur
Hamilton
Hendricks
Henry
Madison
Monroe
Morgan
Rush

The next Target Market to review is by type of client. Are you a specialist or a generalist? Do you only design retirement homes, or do you design factories, office buildings, hospitals, and schools? Do you only work directly with clients, or do you team with architects, engineers, and construction firms? If you have ever created a SF 254, you should have a good start—Section 10 requires you to break down your firm's projects by government profile code. Perhaps you may decide that these codes are too specific in some instances. That's fine, because if you can keep your client types to a minimum, your plan will be shorter. Prepare two lists. First, type of projects: hospitals, warehouses, collegiate facilities, etc.; or subdivisions, stormwater management, surveying, etc.; or asbestos, lead paint, indoor air quality, etc. Once you have developed your list by type of project, determine the percentage of annual business for which each project type accounts. The next list to make is by who pays your bills. Does 80% of your work come from Uncle Sam and 20% of your work come from private developers? Just because you do a lot of collegiate facilities doesn't mean that the college is picking up the tab. Maybe the state government is the real client.

Target Market by Client Type

- Commercial (e.g., a retailer)
- Corporate (e.g., an office building owner/developer)
- Educational (e.g., a school district or college)
- Federal Government (e.g., GSA or DoD)
- Health Care (e.g., a hospital)
- Industrial (e.g., a manufacturer)
- Local Government (e.g., county government)
- Religious (e.g., a church)
- Residential (e.g., a homeowner)
- State Government (e.g., state DOT or DGS)

Designs-R-Us, Indiana Office

TARGET MARKET BY CLIENT TYPE

1. Architects
2. Local Government
3. State Government
4. Federal Government

Target Market by Building Type

- Airports
- Assembly Plants
- Assisted Living Facilities
- Child Care Centers
- Churches
- Classroom Buildings
- Community Centers
- Computer Buildings
- Correctional Facilities
- Distribution Centers
- Dormitories
- Gymnasiums
- Hospitality Facilities
- Hospitals
- Independent Living Facilities
- Judicial Facilities
- Libraries
- Manufacturing Plants
- Military Installations
- Multi-Family Housing Facilities
- Museums
- Office Buildings
- Performing Arts Centers
- Postal Facilities
- Recreational Facilities
- Research Facilities
- Restaurants
- Retail Facilities
- Transportation Facilities
- Vehicle Maintenance Facilities
- Water Treatment Facilities
- Wastewater Treatment Facilities

Designs-R-Us, Indiana Office

TARGET MARKET BY BUILDING TYPE

1. Correctional Facilities
2. Classroom Buildings
3. Dormitories
4. Office Buildings
5. Postal Facilities
6. Assisted Living Facilities

I'm a big fan of visual aids: charts, graphs, and bullet lists. Create pie charts for your Target Markets. Break down your project locations into regions or states or countries. Do the same for each project type and each client type. You know what they say (and just exactly who are "they," and when did "they" first say it?): A picture is worth a thousand words.

A highly effective way to segment your market can be found in any basic marketing textbook. Create a grid three columns wide by three columns high. Across the top, rank your company strength, based upon the experience of the firm as well as the credentials of your staff. Do you have extensive experience in a certain type of project? If so, that market segment would fall under the "Strong" column. Perhaps your firm isn't highly-credentialed in a certain market segment, but a number of your staff members have a significant background in that segment. If that is the case, rank yourself as "Average." Or, perhaps it is a project type or market in which your firm and staff members have little or no experience. Rank yourself as "Weak."

On the left side of the grid, rank the attractiveness of the market segment. Is it growing? Is it profitable? Is the market large enough to support your firm? If so, the market segment attractiveness is "High." Perhaps the market segment has proven profitable to your firm, but the overall volume of work within that particular market sector is diminishing. This would be a "Medium." And, of course, if there is little work in the market segment, or if your fees are too high to effectively compete, rank it a "Low."

Next, you will need to juxtapose the attractiveness of each market segment with your company strength in that segment. In terms of target markets, you can do this by client type, building type, geographic region, or even by the type of services you offer. In the case of Designs-R-Us, they have found the collegiate market to be growing and profitable—and they have many projects in their portfolio—so they may rank it in the "High-Strong" box. On the other end of the spectrum, perhaps they have found the residential or church market segments to be "Low-Weak": they have limited or no experience in those segments, and their fee structure is far too high to be profitable.

Your primary target markets are the three boxes labeled "A." In most cases, your firm will automatically pursue projects falling within these categories. The three labeled "B" are iffy. You should consider these market segments on a case-by-case basis, perhaps developing a formal Go/No-Go decision making process. Finally, the three "C" boxes are almost always avoided unless a special condition warrants pursuit of a project within the "C" market segments.

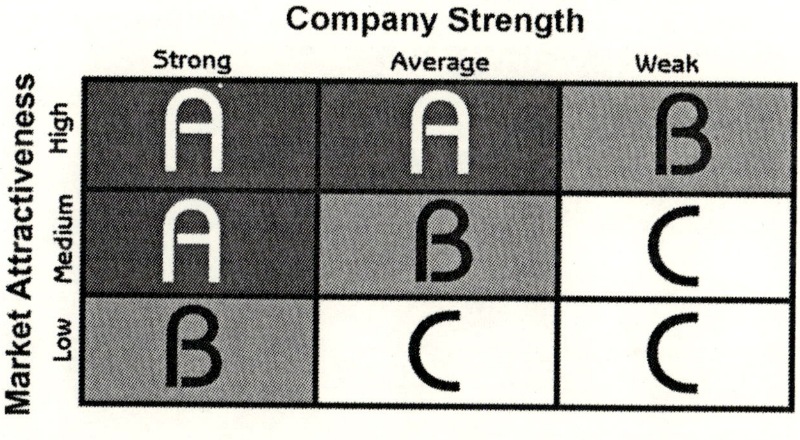

Marketing Responsibilities

Everyone is a marketer, or so the old adage goes. But is that a reality in your firm? This section should define everyone's responsibilities. Is the marketing department solely responsibly for marketing? How does your firm define "marketing"? Are sales and marketing one in the same, or are they different? Do the principals and project managers have a responsibility to contribute to sales and marketing? Is there a marketing committee? Develop a marketing organizational chart that includes all individuals involved in the sales and marketing process. There are many ways to structure a marketing department—even if there is no "real" marketing department! Some firms have a dedicated sales representative who is always on the road. Some have a principal who spends x% of his or her time in sales-related activities. Perhaps all principals are required to spend 40% of their time in sales and marketing, and project managers another 20%. Maybe the marketing manager is the only staff member with sales responsibilities, or maybe only the company president! Define your firm's marketing responsibilities, and name names. These individuals will be responsible for executing the strategies that you develop in the next section.

Business Development Structure

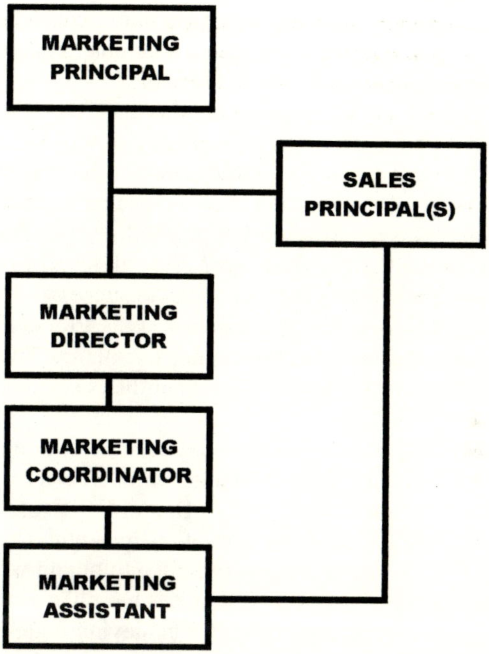

This Year's Marketing Goals & Strategies

At last, the "meat" of the plan, where you determine your destinations and create a customized Trip Tic. These goals and strategies do not have to be based on the calendar year. They don't have to be a year's worth of objectives, either—they can be for a period of six months or a period of two years.

I like to break this section down into a series of sub-plans: Sales Plan, Public Relations Plan, Advertising Plan, Collateral Materials Plan, and Research Plan. Also in this section I add five-year objectives.

Perhaps the single most important portion of your Marketing Plan is the Sales Plan. How much do you need to gross/net this year to stay in business and grow? Note that the figures in this section must be in harmony with the firm's Strategic Plan. While the Strategic Plan may state "net $1,500,000 in bookings," the Marketing Plan must break down these bookings, and how to obtain them. Remember that little section called Target Market? Use the graphs you created to assist you in breaking down the bookings. Maybe last year you received $575,000 from hospitals. In your Situational Analysis you briefly discussed trends (you did, didn't you?). Does the hospital market continue to be active? Is there enough work to support another $575,000 this year? How about $700,000? Will it all come from existing clients, or will $250,000 have to come from new clients? Break down your target sales by geographic region and type of client. Your Target Market section shows those markets in which you have been successful, and those markets in which you haven't. Do you wish to grow in certain markets or walk away from any? This all needs to be determined in the Sales Plan. Now, what are your directions to successfully arrive there? If you have an integrated marketing program—selling, PR, advertising—you will address the non-sales objectives in your other sub-plans. The next step in your Sales Plan is to revisit the Marketing Responsibilities section.

Will personal selling be required (dumb question—of course it will be!)? Who is charged with what? "Project Manger John Doe is responsible for maintaining relationships with Colleges A, B, and C. Also, Project Manager John Doe is responsible for developing relationships with Colleges X, Y, and Z." Be specific. Don't state that you would like to obtain work with five new developers. That may be a good target, but it is merely a goal. How you plan to *achieve* that goal and who is responsible for achieving it are more important. Take each goal, and tell your readers (management staff) how you are going to get there.

(At this time I'd like to digress a tad and discuss the concept of multiple Marketing Plans. As companies grow, and their sales and marketing programs become more sophisticated, it is time to consider preparing several Marketing Plans. This can be done in many ways: by office or region, by client type or project type, or even by discipline or specialty service. General Motors doesn't have just one Marketing Plan—each subsidiary has one. Furthermore, Pontiac doesn't just have one, but each car line does. The Pontiac Grand Am doesn't have just one Marketing Plan, but there is one for each country in which it is sold. You can visualize a pyramid developing. Note that there is still one overall corporate Marketing Plan from which the other, more specific Marketing Plans emerge. Most professional services firms only need one, but don't be afraid to create specialty Marketing Plans; after all, you need to know how to get where you're going if you ever expect to reach your destination!)

If you subscribe to the philosophy that each individual charged with selling should have contact goals, then this is the place to put them: "Principal Jones must make twenty contacts with prospective clients per month and fifteen contacts with existing clients per month." Note how this is specific and—new word, folks—measurable. If you recall, earlier we mentioned that one of the main reasons for not achieving the previous year's objectives is the lack of a formal strategy. And for a strategy to be evaluated in terms of success/failure, it must be measurable. "Obtain $2,200,000 from health care clients" is measurable; "Further penetrate the hospital market" is not.

Once you have developed your sales goals by client type or project type or region or discipline or all of the above, you are ready to move on to the Public Relations Plan.

What do you plan to achieve from a PR standpoint over the course of the next year? Are you going to prepare five press releases per month and mail them to a list of twenty periodicals? Are you going to hold two educational seminars for clients? Is each principal and project manager going to give one speech to a trade or client organization? If so, which principals, what topic, and where? Likewise, are you going to attempt to be published? Are internal staff going to prepare the article(s), or are you going to hire an outside consultant? What are potential topics and publications? Of course, with speeches and publications you have no guarantee of success, but by creating a list of potential speeches on potential topics to potential audiences, you have a written reminder of the goal. Next, develop a list of steps that can be taken: "Contact *x* magazines about *y* topics; contact *x* organizations about *y* presentations."

Another valuable PR tool is civic involvement. Really, everyone in the company should seek to volunteer their time to a community group or client organization. Furthermore, becoming active on committees and boards has two great benefits: first, you are doing a service to the community; second, the community (and other like-minded business people) will view you and your firm as socially responsible. Make a list of potential organizations, and who should become involved with them. "By June of this year, Jane Doe will become active in the local United Way chapter" is certainly a specific objective.

Designs-R-Us, Indiana Office

PUBLIC RELATIONS PLAN

1. Press Releases
Prepare at least one press release every other month for distribution to our media mailing list. Topics should include personnel (new hires, promotions, licenses obtained, awards received, speeches given, articles published), projects (new contracts, ground-breaking ceremonies, design awards), or any other topic deemed newsworthy. Our current mailing list includes:

- *Newspaper A*
- *Newspaper B*
- *Newspaper C*
- *Business Journal D*
- *Business Journal E*
- *Regional Magazine X*
- *Regional Magazine Y*
- *National Magazine Z*

Responsibility:
Joanna Mellancamp, Marketing Manager
Timeframe:
Bi-Monthly

2. Presentations
Each principal should, at a minimum, participate on one panel or give one presentation to a client group. The marketing department will assist each principal in targeting organizations and preparing the speech.

Responsibility:
Joanna Mellancamp, Marketing Manager
- research and presentation development
John Smith, Principal
- health care organizations
Jane Doe, Principal
- collegiate organizations
Ima Rich, Principal
- K-12 organizations
Timeframe:
1 presentation every four months

3. Articles
Each principal should, at a minimum, write one article for publication in a client or trade periodical. Like presentations, published articles enhance our corporate image. The marketing department will be responsible for researching publications, querying editors, and ghostwriting the articles.

Responsibility:
Joanna Mellancamp, Marketing Manager
- research, queries, ghost writing
John Smith, Principal
- health care periodicals
Jane Doe, Principal
- collegiate periodicals
Ima Rich, Principal
- K-12 periodicals
Timeframe:
1 article every four months

4. Contests
Designs-R-Us will enter two design contests during the course of the year. Project X will be entered in the annual ASHRAE contest, and Project Y in the annual IEEE contest.

Responsibility:
Joanna Mellancamp, Marketing Manager
Timeframe:
ASHRAE – July; IEEE – September

5. Facilities
We will make our facilities available for non-profit organizations needing conferencing and training space. We have done this in the past and typically allow three organizations to use our conference room.

Responsibility:
Joanna Mellancamp, Marketing Manager
Timeframe:
As requested

Another important component of the year's objectives is the Collateral Materials (a.k.a., Corporate Communications, Marketing Materials) Plan. Outline what you plan to create, print, mail, update, etc. Some examples: "Print four issues of *Company Newsletter*; mail on Jan 15, April 15, July 15, October 15." "Develop two four-color tri-fold brochures on *Service A* and *Service B*. Have printed by May 30." "Update SF 254 by June 1." "Create focused SF 254s for military, postal, and court facilities; complete by Sept. 15."

Are you going to print project data sheets? For which projects? Full color or black and white? When will they be ready to distribute? Will you need to purchase a new computer, scanner, or new software? By making a list of items, it becomes much easier to develop the Marketing Budget. Remember, if the budget doesn't support your goals, you can always revise those goals.

Designs-R-Us, Indiana Office

COLLATERAL MATERIALS PLAN

1. Company Newsletter
Print four issues of our company newsletter, "On Design," during the course of the year. Editorial calendar is as follows:

Q1 – Air Quality
Q2 – Anniversary
Q3 – Power Quality
Q4 – Year in Review

Responsibility:
Joanna Mellancamp, Marketing Manager
Timeframe:
1 per quarter

2. Brochures
Print one new four-color trifold brochure targeting the collegiate market.

Responsibility:
Joanna Mellancamp, Marketing Manager
Timeframe:
April 15 (draft); May 15 (final)

3. Project Descriptions
Develop new color project descriptions sheets for the following:

a. Project X
b. Project Y
c. Project Z

Responsibility:
Joanna Mellancamp, Marketing Manager
Timeframe:
February 15 completion

4. Staff Resumes
Update all professional resumes with projects completed over the past year as well as information on continuing education, speeches given, articles written, professional organization activities, and

community/volunteer involvement.

Responsibility:
Joanna Mellancamp, Marketing Manager
Timeframe:
July 1

5. Testimonial Letters
Obtain testimonial letters from two clients—one college and one school district.

Responsibility:
John Smith, Jane Doe
Timeframe:
Q3

6. Project Photography
Obtain professional photographs of the following projects, as they are completed:

a. Project X
b. Project Y
c. Project Z

We will contact the project architect and contractor(s) to invite them to share the costs associated with the photography.

Responsibility:
Joanna Mellancamp
Timeframe:
As projects are completed

7. Direct Mail
Conduct a minimum of one targeted direct mail campaign per quarter to increase name recognition among prospective clients. Campaigns include:

1. Colleges (Marion, Johnson, Shelby Counties)
2. K-12 (Monroe, Brown, Morgan, Hendricks Counties)
3. Architects (Marion, Hamilton, Madison Counties)
4. SF-254 Updates (Entire Mailing List)

Responsibility:
Joanna Mellancamp
Timeframe:
1 per quarter

8. Web Site
Redesign Web site with new logo and company colors; add this year's newsletters to the archive section.

Responsibility:
Joanna Mellancamp
Timeframe:
3Q

Next is the Advertising Plan, if needed. Maybe the only advertising you normally do is in the yellow pages. Maybe you plan to conduct a national advertising campaign in several client publications. If so, which publications? What size ad? Are you planning to advertise in local papers or regional business journals? When? Engineers Week? If you have target periodicals, try to obtain an editorial calendar and rate schedule, so you will know when to advertise and how much it will cost you. Direct mail is another form of advertising. If you mail a generic piece to several thousand clients and prospects, it is advertising. If you send personalized, targeted pieces, they are considered collateral materials.

Designs-R-Us, Indiana Office

ADVERTISING PLAN

1. Yellow Pages
Renew our box ad under "Engineers-Consulting" in the Indianapolis-Suburban East and Hancock County directories.

Responsibility:
Joanna Mellancamp
Timeframe:
Upon receipt of renewal notification

2. MAPPA
Place one full-page ad in the MAPPA annual conference program.

Responsibility:
Joanna Mellancamp
Timeframe:
May

3. ISPE
Place one business-card sized ad in the ISPE annual directory.

Responsibility:
Joanna Mellancamp
Timeframe:
October

The next plan to develop is the Marketing Research Plan. To achieve some of the sales goals, you may be required to conduct extensive market research. Perhaps one of your goals is to move into a new region and work for industrial firms within that market. First, you need to research prospective clients. Maybe you want to obtain a state directory of manufacturers and determine all printing firms within a four-county radius that employ a minimum of 250 workers. This is an aspect of research. Once you have identified these firms, you need to find out more about them, and who the appropriate contact is. Research your competitors. To successfully market against the competition, you have to know the competition. Monitoring of periodicals is an aspect of marketing research. Every once in awhile you may obtain a lead; but more often than not, you can learn about companies: Which firms are growing, laying off, or being acquired? You can also research trends in the markets you serve and in the economy as a hole. Again, be specific. Which periodicals are to be monitored, and which individuals within your organization are charged with monitoring them?

Designs-R-Us, Indiana Office

MARKET RESEARCH PLAN

1. Higher Education Directory
Obtain updated copy of "Indiana Directory of Higher Education."

Responsibility:
Joanna Mellancamp
Timeframe:
1Q

2. Architectural Firms
Research non-client architectural firms in the following counties: Marion, Hamilton, Madison. Obtain contact information for principal in charge of marketing.

Responsibility:
Joanna Mellancamp
Timeframe:
2Q

3. Publications
Continue to subscribe to the following publications:

a. *Indianapolis Business Journal*
b. *Indiana Real Estate Digest*
c. *Indianapolis Star*

Begin subscribing to:

a. *Eastern Indiana Business Journal*

Responsibility:
Joanna Mellancamp
Timeframe:
Renewals as received; *EIBJ* by April 1.

Finally, develop a list of long-term objectives. These are long-term, so you don't have to be too specific. Maybe in five years you want to obtain 30% of your work from Antarctica (the continent's not overbuilt, you know?). Under the sales goals section in the current plan, perhaps you will outline objectives and strategies for obtaining 5% of this year's work from Antarctica. Maybe you want to expand the marketing staff by one person when the amount of gross bookings exceeds $3,000,000. A lot of these objectives will come from your corporate retreat (you know—that strategic planning meeting that the managers are supposed to conduct at least once a year!).

Designs-R-Us, Indiana Office

LONG TERM MARKETING OBJECTIVES

1. Architectural Scales
Obtain architectural scales with company logo and colors to use as handouts for clients and A-List prospective clients.

Timeframe: 1 Year

2. Marketing Software
Purchase Acrobat software to enable Designs-R-Us to save files in PDF format for easy distribution across the Internet.

Timeframe: 1 – 2 Years

3. Computer Projector
Purchase a portable computer project for use in project presentations, client seminars, and staff training.

Timeframe: 2 Years

Executive Summary

Now that your Marketing Plan is developed, it is time to prepare the Executive Summary (translation: the executives are too lazy—uh...busy—to read the full plan, so they need a summary—the abridged version). Since I try to make my Marketing Plan as user-friendly as possible, I like to take every goal and make one sentence out of it. I then create a bullet list of goals (this is only a summary, don't list strategies) and that becomes my Executive Summary. Not only is it quick, easy reading, but it is also a great reference tool. Make extra copies and share it with all staff members.

Note that even though the Executive Summary is prepared last, it should be the first section in the Marketing Plan. You will have a lot of information to cover, so keep your verbiage to a minimum. Charts, graphics and bullet lists work wonders. Also, apply the same design principals to your Marketing Plan that you do to your proposals and qualification submissions. Don't use a "typewriter" font with no Desktop Publishing. You need to "sell" the plan internally, so assume the management staff is your client—you want to be sure to gain and keep their attention.

Designs-R-Us, Indiana Office

EXECUTIVE SUMMARY

Marketing goals for the year include:

1. Public Relations Objectives
- Prepare/distribute a minimum of six news releases
- Conduct at least three presentations to client groups
- Prepare three articles for client/trade periodicals
- Enter two design contests
- Make our conference space available for non-profit groups

2. Collateral Materials Objectives
- Prepare four issues of "On Design" newsletter
- Print one collegiate-oriented 4c tri-fold brochure
- Develop new project description sheets for three projects
- Update professional resumes
- Obtain two testimonial letters
- Obtain professional photographs of three projects
- Conduct four direct mail campaigns
- Redesign Web site; update newsletter archives

3. Advertising Objectives
- Renew Yellow Pages advertisements
- Advertise in MAPPA annual conference program
- Advertise in ISPE annual directory

4. Market Research Objectives
- Obtain updated copy of "Indiana Directory of Higher Ed."
- Research prospective architectural clients in three counties
- Continue to subscribe to business/trade publications

5. Long Term Objectives
- Purchase architectural scales for sales promotion
- Obtain copy of Adobe Acrobat to create PDF files
- Purchase computer projector for presentations and training

SAMPLE MARKETING PLAN FORMAT

1. Executive Summary
2. Table of Contents
3. Situational Analysis
4. Target Market
    - Geographic
    - Client Type
    - Project Type
5. Marketing Responsibilities
6. Evaluation of Previous Goals
7. Objectives/Strategies for This Year
    - Sales Plan
    - Public Relations Plan
    - Collateral Materials Plan
    - Advertising Plan
    - Market Research Plan
8. Appendix: Marketing Budget

This first plan is always the most difficult. However, it is imperative that you don't fall into the trap that so many of us have: avoid the temptation to use the same plan every year, changing only the dates! For a marketing plan to be effective, it must also be dynamic. Review the plan quarterly, and make adjustments if need be. Also, don't keep the plan locked away, hidden from all of your coworkers. Everyone in your firm with some hand in the business development process should have a copy readily available.

Fifty-five hundred words ago I began to travel toward my destination—this paragraph. Hopefully you have enjoyed the ride and found my directions helpful. I've now reached my destination—hopefully you will reach yours, too!

Sales Planning for Professional Services Firms

A Sales Plan is perhaps the most important plan you will ever develop for your business, but in the A/E/C industry, sales planning resources seem to be lacking. This was true ten years ago when I first got into the business, and it still holds true today. In fact, I recently decided to totally revamp my sales plan—out with the old in with the new. I had been doing the same thing for years and—because I'm always preaching about the importance of dynamic plans—it seemed that I needed to better practice what I was preaching. Yet, when I attempted to locate industry benchmarks, I had little luck. In fact, I have an entire library of professional services marketing and management resources; however, they were of minimal use when it came time to develop contact goals and sales forecasts.

Undeterred, I took the "old," heavily modified it, and the "new" was born. Throughout *Sales Planning for Professional Services Firms* we will follow the sales planning process for a hypothetical firm, Designs-R-Us. To create a successful sales plan for your company, follow the recommended *process*; note, however, that the numbers and ratios *are only* for our hypothetical firm—your actual numbers should be based on the historical experience of your firm. This report is merely a benchmark. And if you're just starting out, well, I hope you find the Designs-R-Us plan to be well-reasoned. Look at your market, and do your best to "guesstimate" your numbers. Year 1 is always the most difficult. As you start to collect data—month-to-month, year-to-year—your goals and ratios will become far easier to formulate.

Market Segmentation

Before you can develop your sales goals/forecasts and corresponding contact goals, you should define your market segments. There are many ways you can segments your markets. Here are four:

Geographic Markets

- Region A (City, County, Metropolitan Area, State, or Country)
- Region B (City, County, Metropolitan Area, State, or Country)
- Region C (City, County, Metropolitan Area, State, or Country)

Note that the Geographic Market Segmentation Model can be tailored to multi-office companies. In this case, each Region could represent the geographic territory of a particular office. Geographic segmentation is useful when developing sales goals for individual offices; however, this type of segmentation is of little value when targeting client or industry types.

Client Types

- Commercial (e.g., a retailer)
- Corporate (e.g., an office building owner/developer)
- Educational (e.g., a school district or college)
- Federal Government (e.g., GSA or DoD)
- Health Care (e.g., a hospital)
- Industrial (e.g., a manufacturer)
- Local Government (e.g., county government)
- Religious (e.g., a church)
- Residential (e.g., a homeowner)
- State Government (e.g., state DOT or DGS)

I have a colleague who believes that these categories are far too broad—in his mind, there are only three types of clients: commercial, institutional, and industrial. Everything else is a sub-category.

The Client Type Segmentation Model defines the market by the type of organization paying the bills. For business development purposes, it is more useful than the Geographic Market Segmentation Model because it is more focused on a market or industry.

Building Types

- Airports
- Assembly Plants
- Assisted Living Facilities
- Child Care Centers
- Churches
- Classroom Buildings
- Community Centers
- Computer Buildings
- Correctional Facilities
- Distribution Centers
- Dormitories
- Gymnasiums
- Hospitality Facilities
- Hospitals
- Independent Living Facilities
- Judicial Facilities
- Libraries
- Manufacturing Plants
- Military Installations
- Multi-Family Housing Facilities
- Museums
- Office Buildings
- Performing Arts Centers
- Postal Facilities
- Recreational Facilities
- Research Facilities
- Restaurants
- Retail Facilities
- Transportation Facilities
- Vehicle Maintenance Facilities
- Water Treatment Facilities
- Wastewater Treatment Facilities

As you can see, the Building Type Segmentation Model is far more detailed than the Client Type Segmentation Model. This model allows you to focus on a type of *project* rather than a type of client. In reality, you will most likely use a combination of both models—your sales force needs direction regarding not only which type of organizations to target, but also which type of projects to market to those prospects.

For instance, you may decide to pursue classroom buildings (Project Type) for state-owned universities (Client Type). In this case, you may pursue collegiate work through the state government's department of general services.

However, you may decide to *not* pursue performing arts centers (Project Type) for state-owned universities (Client Type), but still pursue performing arts centers (Project Type) for privately-owned colleges (Client Type).

Likewise, consider distribution centers. A distribution center (Project Type) may be owned by an industrial firm (Client Type—Industrial), a military installation (Client Type—Federal Government), or department store (Client Type—Commercial).

As you can see, there is no "one size fits all" approach to segmenting your market. Perhaps this explains the lack of sales planning resources in the A/E/C industry!

Note that "Building Types" can be easily replaced with "Project Types." Perhaps your firm designs highways and bridges, and also pursues the municipal engineering market.

Further, there is another way to segment your markets:

Services Provided

- Architecture
- Bid Construction
- Civil Engineering
- Construction Management
- Cost Estimating
- Design-Build Construction
- Electrical Engineering
- Facility Management
- Fire Protection Engineering
- Geology
- HVAC Engineering
- Interior Design
- Landscape Architecture
- Negotiated Construction
- Plumbing Engineering
- Program Management
- Scheduling
- Structural Engineering
- Surveying

Obviously, your service mix won't exactly match the sample Services Provided Segmentation Model. However, you can easily see how the waters can get even more muddied!

Many companies have overall corporate sales goals, as well as sales goals for each department. Sometimes, a department works as part of the overall project team and sometimes the department works independently. For instance, a multi-discipline firm may utilize their in-house survey crew as part of a larger project; other times, the crew may work directly for a homeowner.

Only you can segment the appropriate markets for your firm.

Let's look at an example of how confusing segmentation can become. My hypothetical company, Designs-R-Us, is a multi-discipline engineering firm with offices in three locations. Here's an overview of each office:

Pennsylvania Office

Employees:	22
Services:	Structural Engineering Geology Surveying Civil Engineering
Client Types:	Architects (This office only works as subconsultants to architectural firms)
Project Types:	Airports Rail Terminals Bus Stations

Indiana Office

Employees:	8
Services:	HVAC Engineering Electrical Engineering Plumbing Engineering Fire Protection Engineering
Client Types:	Architects Local Government State Government Federal Government
Project Types:	Correctional Facilities Classroom Buildings Dormitories Office Buildings Postal Facilities Assisted Living Facilities

Texas Office

Employees:	52
Services:	Civil Engineering Structural Engineering Electrical Engineering Surveying Landscape Architecture Geology
Client Types:	Local Government State Government
Project Types:	Highways Bridges Roads Municipal Engineer Contracts

Designs-R-Us is quite diverse, with each office having its own specialty. There is some overlap between the offices in terms of services offered, but for the most part they have their own unique markets. There is absolutely no way a "one size fits all" plan can work for Designs-R-Us. Each office (geographic region) requires a customized segmentation plan.

The Pennsylvania office (Geographic Market) sales effort is actually very focused: because this office only works for architects, the most obvious market segment to target is architectural firms (Client Type) that design transportation facilities (Project Type) but do not have structural, civil, survey, or geology resources (Services Provided) in-house.

For simplicity sake, this report will focus on the Indiana office of Designs-R-Us.

Sales Goals

There are two ways to track your sales: billings and bookings. A billing is a realized booking.

Basically, your billings are your revenues. The work has been contracted, services have been performed, and the client has been billed (and hopefully *paid* that bill in a timely fashion). A booking, on the other hand, is work that has been awarded and contracted, but not necessarily billed. Not all bookings become billings—projects die or get delayed, scopes change, etc. In addition, booked work builds backlog, and much of the booked work will become a realized sale (a billing) in the next fiscal year. As a result, your booking goals should always be higher than your billing goals.

So how do you set your sales goals? Let's formulate sales goals for the Indiana office of Designs-R-Us. The office has a total staff complement of eight. Industry metrics tell us that typical professional services firms need at least $85,000 per employee to be profitable, so 8 x $85,000 = $680,000. However, Designs-R-Us recently updated their strategic plan and set a goal of adding one technical staff member. If they are to do this over the course of the next year, they will need to add another $85,000 in revenues (or a prorated amount, depending upon when during the year the hire occurs).

Because the new hire is only a goal, we will keep the billings target the same: $680,000.

However, the bookings goal must reflect the new hire, so our base bookings goal is $765,000 (9 employees at $85,000 per employee). But we also know that not all booked work will become a reality. Let us assume that past experience has taught us that approximately 85% of work booked actually materialized. (Your personal experience may be higher or lower.) In order to have a staff of nine people, we need revenues of $765,000; however, only 85% of the work we book will become a reality, so we divide $765,000 by .85 to get a new bookings goal of $900,000.

Next, we need to look at where this $900,000 is going to come from.

Fortunately, the services offered at the Indiana office of Designs-R-Us are fairly limited—M/E/P engineering. And, the majority of our contracts are for all disciplines. As a result, we decide *not* to segment our bookings goals by services provided. (If we did, we may target 35% of work for the HVAC discipline, 35% of work for the electrical discipline, 20% of work for the plumbing discipline, and 10% of work for the fire protection discipline. These numbers need to reflect the current staff composition, projected future staff composition, and historical billings for each discipline.)

After reviewing our billings from the past five years, we determine that a full 60% of our volume comes via the architectural community. Another 20% come from the state government, with 10% of billings from both the federal government and local governments.

We are further able to determine that 80% of our annual work comes from repeat clients. However, this 80% has only been enough to sustain our staff of eight—if we are to successfully meet the goal of increasing our staff size by one, we will need to increase our volume of work with new clients.

For simplicity, assume that all of the work for the new hire will have to come from new clients. In reality, we need to increase our billings by $85,000; however, we will need to book $100,000 for this new hire in order to account for unrealized sales (which we've already determined averages 15% of bookings).

If our bookings goal last year was based upon eight people at $100,000 per person ($85,000 required per employee + $15,000 for unrealized sales), and 80% of that goal—$640,000—was from repeat clients, with the remaining 20%—$160,000—from new clients, then we can easily develop our goal for this year. Since all work to support the new employee will have to come from new clients, we take the $100,000 goal for that person plus last year's new client goal of $160,000 for a revised goal of $260,000 from new clients and $640,000 from repeat clients. And yes, the math does add up: $260,000 + $640,000 = $900,000.

We can now start to fill in a table:

Client Type	Repeat Bookings	New Bookings	Total Bookings
Architects (60%)			$540,000
State Gov. (20%)			$180,000
Fed. Gov. (10%)			$90,000
Local Gov. (10%)			$90,000
Total (100%)	$640,000	$260,000	$900,000

We must now look at our past history and talk with current clients to determine which segment(s) will constitute the increased bookings. We already know our goals for each client type as well as our goals for new and repeat work; however, back-filling the more detailed breakdown of those goals is an educated guess—especially if you have never done so before.

The Indiana office of Designs-R-Us has had fairly consistent results year-to-year. While the addition of one staff member will allow us to take on more work—or larger projects—the staffing increase is probably not enough to warrant any expectation of more work from the state, federal, or local governments. More likely, the work will come from the architectural community—in fact, we may very well only need one new architectural client to account for the additional $100,000 in bookings.

If this is the case, though, we will have to revisit our earlier percentage goals of 60% of work from architects, 20% of work from state government, 10% of work from federal government, and 10% of work from local government.

If our bookings goal had remained at $800,000, the target bookings would have been as follows:

Architects (60%)	$480,000
State Gov. (20%)	$160,000
Federal Gov. (10%)	$ 80,000
Local Gov. (10%)	$ 80,000

Since we have decided to keep our government bookings goals unchanged, $100,000 in new work must come from the architectural community, bringing the total up to $580,000, or roughly 64% of our overall goal. As a result, our government goals, as a percentage of the overall goal, will each slightly decrease. The revised percentage goals are approximately 18% for state government, 9% for federal government, and 9% for local government. Taking what we now know into consideration, here is our revised table:

Client Type	Repeat Bookings	New Bookings	Total Bookings
Architects (64%)		$100,000	$580,000
State Gov. (18%)			$160,000
Federal Gov. (9%)			$80,000
Local Gov. (9%)			$80,000
Total (100%)	$640,000	$260,000	$900,000

At this point in the process, we still need to determine how much work will come from new clients. Yes, we already have $100,000 to account for the new hire built into our breakdown; however, we still need to determine where the additional $160,000 is going to come from. Because our leading client type is architectural firms—and because we are going to have to target several firms just to get the initial $100,000 increase—it is a logical assumption that we will need to book more than $100,000 from new architectural clients.

In order to determine the repeat client – new client numbers for the three governmental client types, we will use our old 80/20 ratio of repeat work to new work. Based upon this, we can backfill in our table for state, federal, and local governmental bookings (numbers are rounded):

Client Type	Repeat Bookings	New Bookings	Total Bookings
Architects (64%)	$?	$100k +$?	$580,000
State Gov. (18%)	$128,000	$32,000	$160,000
Federal Gov. (9%)	$64,000	$16,000	$80,000
Local Gov. (9%)	$64,000	$16,000	$80,000
Total (100%)	$640,000	$260,000	$900,000

Next, we back out the remaining dollar amounts needed to complete the table. For bookings with repeat architectural clients, our number is: $640,000 – [$128,000 + $64,000 + $64,000] = $384,000. Likewise, for bookings with new architectural clients, our number is $260,000 – [$32,000 + $16,000 + $16,000] = $196,000. And remember, $100,000 of that $196,000 goal was previously accounted for. Here is our new table:

Client Type	Repeat Bookings	New Bookings	Total Bookings
Architects (64%)	$384,000	$196,000	$580,000
State Gov. (18%)	$128,000	$32,000	$160,000
Federal Gov. (9%)	$64,000	$16,000	$80,000
Local Gov. (9%)	$64,000	$16,000	$80,000
Total (100%)	$640,000	$260,000	$900,000

Amazingly, it even adds up!

Now that we have developed our goals, we need to look at each individual goal to determine if it is realistic. For instance, can our existing architectural client base support $384,000 in bookings? Can we realistically expect to book $32,000 from a new state government client?

Since our Indiana office is fairly small, we only work with the Indiana state government, and not the governments of the neighboring states. However, while we have booked projects with the Indiana Public Works Division, we have never worked directly with the Purdue University. Therefore, we will target the institution for new state government bookings (the university is state-owned).

Also, note that the $16,000 goals for both new federal government and new local government bookings are almost too small to warrant much proactive marketing effort. However, the mere fact that we have a goal forces us to consider that market in our sales strategy. Further, the unique goals which you develop for your firm will probably have significantly higher amounts, especially if your firm is larger than eight or nine people!

This is a very basic example to assist you with developing your plans. We just as easily could have created our table based upon building (or project) types:

Building Type	Repeat Bookings	New Bookings	Total Bookings
Correctional Fac.			
Classroom Bldgs.			
Dormitories			
Office Buildings			
Postal Facilities			
Assisted Living Fac.			
Total (100%)	$640,000	$260,000	$900,000

Contact Goals

The Indiana office of Designs-R-Us now has some realistic, measurable sales (bookings) goals. Next, we must determine our business development strategy in terms of sales contacts.

Some firms subscribe to the notion that there should be written contact goals. If you seek to develop contact goals as well, here are a few techniques you can utilize to develop those goals.

Based upon historical data, determine the average size project for each client type. At Designs-R-Us, we've evaluated our past billings, and determined the following averages:

	Average Revenue Per Project	
Client Type	Existing Client	New Client
Architects	$60,000	$35,000
State Government	$55,000	$42,000
Federal Gov.	$70,000	$26,000
Local Government	$14,000	$8,000

In order to determine our sales contact requirements, we are going to use some basic assumptions. First, we need to contact an existing client at least four times per year. Obviously, if we have an active project with that client, there will be many more contacts. However, these four contacts should be "above and beyond" project-related contacts. These are contacts to say hello, see how things are going, see if there are any other projects coming down the pike, etc. Of these four contacts, one should be a personal visit, two should be via the telephone, and one should be networking-related (e.g., a society or chamber of commerce meeting).

Next, we are going to assume that we will have to contact fifty prospects to get one new client. (Note that this is a "generic" industry metric—depending upon the economy and how focused your marketing is, your ratio may be 100:1 or 25:1. Since I'm trying to illustrate a simple example, I'll use 50:1.) For every 50 prospects, we will identify ten "qualified" prospects; that is, organizations that hire firms like Designs-R-Us and are not under a long-term contract with a competitor. Further, five of these ten will have an actual project for which they need a design professional. Of these five, we can realistically expect to get one contract.

So, 50 prospects for 10 qualified prospects for 5 potential projects for 1 contract.

(Because Designs-R-Us does most of its work with architects, the ratios should actually be significantly lower—as a subconsultant, their architectural client would actually handle most of the business development activities.)

Forty of the 50 will be one-time contacts. We will determine that there is no need to maintain contact with them—they don't need a firm like ours, they have a long-term contract with a competitor, they have staff engineers, etc. The five qualified prospects will require four contacts per year, similar to the existing client contact structure. The remaining five prospects will need to be contacted bi-monthly (or monthly or weekly, depending upon how close the project is to becoming a reality). Here are our corresponding contact goals:

- 40 dead-end prospects – 1 telephone
- 5 qualified prospects with no active project – 1 personal, 2 telephone, 1 networking
- 5 qualified prospects with active project – 2 personal, 3 telephone, 1 networking

The next step in the planning process is to cross-reference the average revenue per project with the number of contacts required to obtain one contract. For instance, our goal for repeat work with architectural clients is $384,000, with an average billing of $60,000 per project. We know that we will need 6.4 projects to reach our goal ($384,000/$60,000), so we will use 7 projects as our target. We previously determined that we need 2 phone, 1 personal, and 1 networking contact per year with each existing client. Our corresponding goals are as follows:

- 2 telephone contacts x 7 projects = 14 telephone contacts
- 1 personal contact x 7 projects = 7 personal contacts
- 1 networking contact x 7 projects = 7 networking contacts

Obviously, this is a very basic formula. Perhaps only two clients account for all of your work. Perhaps there are different client contacts within that same firm. Again, only you can determine the appropriate formula for your company.

On the new architectural client side, we already know that we will need $196,000 in bookings, and the each booking will average $35,000, based upon historical data. Thus, we will need 5.6 projects, so our target becomes 6. Here's where things get a bit more complex.

Dead End Prospects

- 40 prospects x 1 telephone x 6 projects = 240 telephone contacts

Qualified Prospects – No Active Project

- 5 prospects x 1 personal contact x 6 projects = 30 personal contacts
- 5 prospects x 2 telephone contacts x 6 projects = 60 telephone contacts
- 5 prospects x 1 networking contact x 6 projects = 30 networking contacts

Qualified Prospects – Active Project

- 5 prospects x 2 personal contacts x 6 projects = 60 personal contacts
- 5 prospects x 3 telephone contacts x 6 projects = 90 telephone contacts
- 5 prospects x 1 networking contact x 6 projects = 30 networking contacts

Remember, we started with fifty prospects for that one project, and we need six projects. To set our goals, we must add all required personal contacts (30 + 60), all required telephone contacts (240 + 60 + 90), and all required networking contacts (30 + 30). The contact goals add up very quickly!

By dividing the bookings goals for each client type by the average revenue per project for each client type, we determine that we need the following number of projects (every number is rounded up to the nearest whole number):

	Number of Projects Required	
Client Type	Existing Client	New Client
Architects	7	6
State Government	3	1
Federal Govern.	1	1
Local Government	5	2

After we use these same contact formulas for all market segments, we are able to develop the following table:

	Required Contacts						
	Repeat Clients			New Clients			
Client Type	Per.	Tel.	Net.	Per.	Tel.	Net.	Totals
Architects	7	14	7	90	390	60	568
State Gov.	3	6	3	15	65	10	102
Federal Gov.	1	2	1	15	65	10	94
Local Gov.	5	10	5	30	130	20	200
Totals	16	32	16	150	650	100	964

Wow—964 contacts!

Depending upon your market and geographic area, as well as the local economic conditions, these formulas may be realistic—or, they may comprise a "shotgun" approach! It is also important to note that the Indiana office of Designs-R-Us is a pretty small firm serving a relatively narrow geographic radius. Are there 300 prospective architectural clients within that radius, much less 50 state, 50 federal, and 100 local government prospects? I seriously doubt it. But hey—we're in Hypothetical Land, so let's continue…

Assuming that these contact goals are realistic, we must now determine the time commitment required to meet these goals. Based upon our history, we determine that an average marketing-related visit with an existing client lasts 2.5 hours, including travel time. Phone conversations typically last about ten minutes. Most of the networking contacts occur at breakfast meetings, lunch meetings, or evening meetings, so we will not include them in our time computations.

We also look at the time commitment required for contacting prospective clients. On average, it takes one hour to prepare for the meeting (including research, brochure preparation, presentation development, etc.), as well as two hours of meeting and travel time. Our time commitment is three hours per personal visit. Further, approximately eight minutes are required for each telephone contact. The conversations are shorter than those we have with existing clients—sometimes a lot shorter—but we must also do a little research before making the call.

Utilizing these basic numbers and simple math, we are able to determine time commitments in hours (for example, 7 personal contacts with existing architectural clients x 2.5 hours/visit = 17.5 hours; 14 telephone contacts with existing architectural clients x 10 minutes/contact = 140 minutes or 2.3 hours):

	Time Commitment in Hours (Rounded Totals)				
	Repeat		New		
Client Type	Per.	Tel.	Per.	Tel.	Totals
Architects	17.5	2.3	270	52	342
State Gov.	7.5	1	45	8.7	62
Federal Gov.	2.5	.3	45	8.7	56
Local Gov.	12.5	1.7	90	17.3	122
Totals	40	5	450	87	582

In our example, it takes 45 hours of sales effort to book $640,000 of work with existing clients, compared with the 537 hours it takes to book $260,000 with new clients! For those of you doing the math, this means that every hour of effort selling to existing clients should account for over $14,000 in bookings, while every hour of effort spent selling to prospective clients equates to a measly $484 in bookings!

This model emphasizes the importance of partnering with your current clients—keep them happy and they will keep coming back! Further, the more work you can obtain for existing clients, the more you will be able to minimize your sales costs.

So how does this example relate to real hours? A typical employee gets paid for 2080 hours of work per year (40 hours per week x 52 weeks per year). The 582 hours would equate to .28 of an equivalent full-time employee. Of course, there are many other responsibilities that fall under the business development umbrella: market research, collateral material development, public relations, advertising, and—a big time-consumer—proposal development.

There are three principals within the Indiana office of Designs-R-Us, and each is charged with business development tasks. Two of the principals handle the existing accounts (with a minor amount of new business development), and the third principal is charged with new business development. Here's how their time would break down:

<u>Principals—Existing Account Management (2 Principals)</u>

Personal Contacts—Existing:	8 per year 1.7 hours per month
Personal Contacts—New:	24 per year 6 hours per month
Telephone Contacts—Existing:	16 per year 13.3 minutes per month
Telephone Contacts—New:	104 per year 1.2 hours per month
Total Commitment Per Principal:	9.1 hours per month 2.1 hours per week

<u>Principal—New Account Management (1 Principal)</u>

Personal Contacts—New:	102 per year 25.5 hours per month
Telephone Contacts—New:	442 per year 5 hours per month
Total Commitment:	30.5 hours per month 7 hours per week

When you look at the time commitment required, the goal of 964 contacts suddenly seems quite manageable!

It is important to note, however, that the principals charged with existing account management should *not* be required to research prospective clients. They should be given the names and numbers of the contacts to make. Either the third principal—charged with new account management—would have this under his or her responsibilities, or else another individual within the firm charged with market research. Because the Designs-R-Us Indiana office is fairly small, the third principal actually handles most of the marketing, so he or she will assist the other two principals with their selling responsibilities. In fact, this principal will most likely do a lot of the bird-dogging, and bring the other two principals along for personal visits and presentations. This hypothetical example merely illustrates the process to get you started.

Further, the new prospect contacts should never be "cold." Perhaps they are referrals from satisfied clients or vendors, perhaps quality networking contacts, or perhaps the marketing effort has turned a cold contact into a warm one.

Market Segment Action Plans

One tool which I have found very useful is the Market Segment Action Plan. This document is a one or two page plan that summarizes your sales and marketing efforts for a specific market segment, be it a client type, building type, service type, or geographic area. Rather than attempt to explain it, let's look at the Designs-R-Us plan for classroom buildings.

Designs-R-Us, Indiana Office

Market Segment:
Classroom Buildings

Profile Code:
029

Description:
Primary and secondary educational facilities;
Technical schools;
Colleges and universities

Historical Billings:
A. As subconsultant to architects – 14% of annual volume
B. Direct with state government – 12% of annual volume

Booking Goals:
A. As subconsultant to architects
- Percent of total: 20%
- Total Goal: $180,000
  - Repeat: $126,000
  - New: $54,000

B. Direct with state government
- Percent of total: 12%
- Total Goal: $108,000
  - Repeat: $86,400
  - New: $21,600

Contact Goals:
A. Architects
1. Personal
   a. Existing – 2
   b. New – 30
2. Telephone
   a. Existing – 4
   b. New – 130
3. Networking
   a. Existing – 2
   b. New – 20

B. State Government
  1. Personal
    a. Existing – 2
    b. New – 15
  2. Telephone
    a. Existing – 4
    b. New – 65
  3. Networking
    a. Existing – 2
    b. New – 10

Overall Responsibility
A. Existing – Jane Doe, PE, Principal
B. New – John Smith, Principal

Organizations
A. Active Membership
  Midwest APPA
B. Potential Membership
  Association of Higher Education Facilities Officers
  Indiana AASA

Identified Projects
A. Hancock County Schools (Existing Client)
  Middle School Expansion
    Amount: $6,200,000
    Timeframe: 3Q
    Account Manager: Jane Doe, PE
  Elementary School Boiler Replacement
    Amount: $550,000
    Timeframe: 2Q
    Account Manager: Jane Doe, PE
B. Indianapolis Community College (Prospective Client)
  New Classroom Building
    Amount: $18,000,000
    Timeframe: 4Q
    Account Manager: John Smith

This simplified market segment action plan demonstrates an easy way to summarize both your activities and opportunities within each market segment. You may want to expand upon the plan and add the complementary marketing activities that will be required. For instance, target five new school districts and ten new institutional architects; develop a direct mail campaign to introduce your firm, develop name recognition, and increase awareness; print one four-color brochure highlighting your classroom building design experience; send one staff member for technology design training and begin to promote this specialty; join one of the two identified organizations; write an article on classroom indoor air quality for *Magazine X*; give a presentation on classroom indoor air quality to *Professional Society Y*. You may have noticed that the actual booking goals were increased over the historical revenues. This was done in order to account for the increased revenue needs associated with the addition of one staff member. Designs-R-Us feels that some of that work will come from the classroom building segment.

Account Management & Tracking

For your business development program to be successful, you must have a formalized tracking and reporting system. There are several software programs—like Act and Goldmine—that were developed specifically for contact management. Or, you can customize a database program like Access to suite your needs. Regardless, here is the basic information you should track:

<u>Contact Database</u>

(1) Account Name (company or institution)
(2) Account Number
(3) Account Manager (individual within your firm overseeing the account)

(4) Status
- Existing Client
- Existing Prospect
- New Prospect

(5) Client Type
(6) Street
(7) City
(8) County
(9) State
(10) Country
(11) Telephone
(12) Fax
(13) Web Site
(14) Primary Contact Person
   a. Name
   b. Title
   c. Mailing Address
   d. Telephone
   e. Fax
   f. Cell Phone
   g. E-Mail
   h. Mailing List(s)
      - Newsletter
      - Holiday Card
      - Direct Mail

(15) Secondary Contact Person
   a. Name
   b. Title
   c. Mailing Address
   d. Telephone
   e. Fax
   f. Cell Phone
   g. E-Mail
   h. Mailing List(s)
      - Newsletter
      - Holiday Card
      - Direct Mail

(16) Last Contact Date
(17) Next Contact Date
(18) Notes

This is just a sample of the information you can track. Some sales professionals get very detailed, even personal, with the information they compile. For instance: spouse name, children, hobbies, organizations, colleges attended, etc.

By having everything in a separate field, you can easily perform searches and/or sorts, which is especially helpful if you plan to conduct a direct mailing to a certain client type in a certain geographic area. Each collection of data is known as a report. Here's how a completed report would look for Designs-R-Us:

Designs-R-Us, Indiana Office

ACCOUNT MANAGEMENT REPORT

Account Name:
Really Big College
Account Number:
178
Account Manager:
John Smith
Status:
Existing Prospect
Client Type:
Educational
Street:
123 Pedagogical Avenue
City:
Greenfield
County:
Hancock
State:
Indiana
Country:
USA
Telephone:
(317) 555-5555
Fax:
(317) 555-4444
Primary Contact Person:
Name: Ima Rich
Title: Director, Physical Plant
Mailing Address PO Box 5555
Telephone: (317) 555-5566
Fax: (317) 555-4466
Cell Phone: (317) 555-9876
E-Mail: ima.rich@reallybigcollege.edu
Mailing List: Newsletter
Last Contact Date:
May 28
Next Contact Date:
June 16
Notes:
Tracking a $3.5 million classroom building.

Another important database—that should be linked with the contact database—is the proposal and lead database, which serves as a tool to track potential projects. Perhaps they are only leads at this point—a prospect that may have a need, a project coming down the pike—or maybe they are "real" projects for which you have submitted a proposal or will soon be submitting a proposal. Here is some of the basic information you should track:

Proposal / Lead Database

(1) Proposal/Lead Number
(2) Account Name
(3) Primary Contact
(4) Account Manager
(5) Client Type
(6) Project Type
(7) Project Location
(8) Sales Stage
- Prospect
- Initial Contact
- Meeting
- Proposal
- First Interview
- Second Interview
- Client Review
- Negotiation
- Commitment
- Follow-Up

(9) Next Contact Date
(10) Construction Cost
(11) Award Date
(12) Fee
(13) Probability
(14) Adjusted Fee (based upon probability)

And here is a sample record from the Designs-R-Us proposal database:

Designs-R-Us, Indiana Office

PROPOSAL / LEAD REPORT

Proposal/Lead Number:
01545
Account Name:
Really Big College
Primary Contact:
Ima Rich
Account Manager:
John Smith
Client Type:
Educational
Project Type:
Classroom Building
Project Location:
Greenfield, IN
Sales Stage:
First Interview
Next Contact Date:
June 16
Construction Cost:
$3,500,000
Award Date:
August 1
Fee:
$122,500
Probability:
20%
Adjusted Fee:
$24,500

From each individual record, you can create a report summarizing the current sales activity. You can sort these reports by account manager, award date, client type, project type, or any other method that works for you. The advantage of listing the fee, probability, and adjusted fee is that you can develop a dynamic sales forecast that is always up-to-date. While you may be tracking over $800,000 in potential fees, the adjusted fee number tells you that you can realistically only expect to be awarded $370,000 of that number.

Based on this forecast, you may need to adjust your sales and marketing activities.

Summary

There is no boilerplate plan that is applicable to every firm. In fact, a sales plan that works for one office or division of a company may be totally inappropriate for another office or division.

This report outlines some of the basic techniques and items you can incorporate as you develop your own sales plan. Use it as the benchmark I never had; customize it to your firm's unique environment.

The first sales plan is always the most difficult, but now you don't have to go it alone.

Structuring for Business Development

In the start-up phase of a company, business development usually falls to the owner, president, or principals of the company. As the company grows, the need for a more formal business development manager increases. At what level this occurs is variable, but it must occur when the owner's available time for it becomes too limited. The first business development staff member might be a part-time project manager or a senior estimator.

The role of the business development manager is to find the best balance among all the various marketing functions. Although sales is a major responsibility of this manager, he or she must also be adept at backing up the sales function with the proper mix of public relations, advertising, research, corporate communications, and technical understanding.

The second-level marketing staff member in a larger company should be a business development assistant or coordinator, either full-time or part-time. Time is critical, and without an assistant to take some of the details away from the business development manager, many opportunities may be missed. The role of the assistant is to provide clerical support; conduct research; keep records; write corporate communications, press releases, and proposals; keep schedules; etc. A single office assistant can accomplish all this with the aid of a personal computer and the latest software. Many software packages can provide customized resumes and project experience statements, project proposals, status reports, data on past and current marketing performance, lead follow-up reminders, and other sales features.

Not until the department has a business development manager responsible for all departmental activities, as well as a business development coordinator, should any more sales specialists be assigned. The third hire is usually a full-time field sales specialist who is responsible for locating, contacting, and meeting with qualified clients. Other specialists are brought aboard as necessary, possibly through consultants. Some firms employe sales consultants who represent them to potential clients, on a commission basis, with good results. A few even hire telemarketing firms to set up sales appointments.

The business development umbrella extends beyond department personnel to any employee who has an opportunity to develop new business. In addition to those in the business development department, others with some responsibilities include principals, department heads, estimators, project managers, and field supervisors. Even foremen and journeymen have a role in marketing.

Given that anyone can engage in business development, it is helpful to take the client's perspective when trying to understand the importance of which individuals perform these functions. Ask yourself: If I am conducting final interviews to select a design professional or contractor from the short list, who would I like to see present at the interview? Probably a principal and/or the project manager and lead designer(s). The project manager—as your firm's assigned point of contact—plays a major role in securing repeat business from current clients. Because of their potential for developing business, principals, department heads, and project managers should all have a fairly good understanding of the business development process.

The Basics: Sales

Marketing is often confused with sales, or lumped into the same category. Sales involves contact with a prospect, whether it be in person, via telephone, or during a "cold call" meeting. A good salesperson knows to "create" chance meetings! Networking is an important part of the sales process and, in the long run, can become your most powerful prospecting tool. It provides a mechanism for building relationships that supercede the traditional "me salesperson, you prospect" mentality. Being active in multiple organizations allows contact with literally hundreds of prospects in a non-threatening manner. The ultimate goal is to be perceived as a friendly problem-solver, and not as a "salesperson"—as a consultant, not a promoter.

While networking provides a great opportunity to meet prospects, chances are that a given firm needs more formal sales activities to generate business. The least favorite of these is the "cold-call"—a contact with a potential client not previously contacted. These prospects are usually identified as a result of market research or as a lead picked up from an indirect source.

While statistics vary depending upon the source, it is often said that for every ten contacts, one or two may be "qualified" (have a funded project and are not already committed to a design/construction firm). For every five qualified prospects, one project may result. In other words, you many need to make fifty contacts to secure one contract! Ratios vary from 1:30 in good times to as much as 1:100+ during bad economic times. So many failures for a single success requires a high level of self-esteem and a very positive, optimistic attitude. The salesperson must not consider rejection personally, but merely as a routine part of doing business, and must always assume the next call will result in a contract.

Opportunities and preparation combine to produce sales. Be prepared! You must know your product, your client, and your competition. You must be straightforward. If you don't know the answer to a prospect's question, say so. You must present yourself not as a professional salesperson, but as a competent problem solver.

The Basics: Public Relations

Public relations is a powerful, though underutilized, business development tool. It allows you to shape your corporate image among industry prospects at little or no cost by feeding the media regularly with positive news that you create. News releases are a great way to do this. Send releases on job completions, new hires, seminars, speeches, projects, awards, charitable events, etc. to all newspapers, business journals and electronic media within your geographic target market.

Keep the releases short—three or four paragraphs will usually suffice. Use the "inverted pyramid" style—with the most important information first and the least important information last. Be sure to take the "who-what-why-where-when" news approach when writing the copy.

Make your release "newsworthy." A newspaper won't print a release about Company XYZ hiring a new receptionist, but may print a release on the hiring of a new manager or completion of a major project. Don't "toot your own horn," but tell the story in a way that emphasizes client benefits.

Other common tools of public relations include sponsorships of special events, donations to charitable causes, establishment of a scholarship fund, speeches, seminars, serving on boards, volunteering, and many more. A firm that is known and respected through various community activities will have that extra edge over one that isn't.

The Basics: Marketing Research

The main purposes of marketing (or market) research are to identify prospects and learn as much about them as possible, to develop profiles on all competitors, to research trends, and to locate unfulfilled needs. If an unfulfilled need is located, you can be the first in that particular market and have the niche to yourself until your competitors learn about it. Market research can determine if there is a void, and if the void is worth filling. When done by your industry association, a lot of the duplication in and cost of market research can be saved.

Effective strategic planning must take various trends into account. Is the economy expanding or contracting? Where will the industry be five years from now? Is an increase or decrease in design-build anticipated? Design-bid? Construction management? These are just a few questions that need to be considered while researching trends. Much information can be obtained from trade publications and local chambers of commerce.

To effectively sell against your competitors, you must know them. What services do they offer? How large are they? Who are their clients? What is their reputation? The more you know about them, the better prepared you will be. Information sources include vendors, trade organizations, newspapers, the Internet, project signs, and so forth. Even the Yellow Pages can be helpful.

Finally, market research also includes identifying qualified prospects and learning about them. Leads can come from newspaper articles, networking, vendors, colleagues, project announcements, annual reports, lead services such as the Dodge Reports, and a host of other sources. You must have an adequate target market in order to generate enough leads to fill your prospect lists. Keep an updated file on each prospect. Libraries that contain financial reports are good sources of information for larger firms. Remember, you want to find the key decision-makers with the power to sign purchase orders.

The Basics: Advertising

If your firm is only going to advertise in one place, that one place should probably be the Yellow Pages. The ad need not be elaborate, but *must* contain the company name and phone number under all appropriate headings. Of course, the larger the ad, the more attention it receives. The main purpose of the ad is to make your number easily accessible. If you see a viable market for those who look to the Yellow Pages to select a firm like yours, then by all means take out a larger ad!

Other places to consider advertising are newspapers, business journals, trade publications, and client publications. There is one additional advertisement that can give you a good amount of exposure: The project sign. It should be easily read and displayed at selected project sites that showcase your exceptional qualifications.

The Basics: Collateral Materials

Collateral materials are also known as marketing materials and sales literature. Brochures, mass mailings, and newsletters all fall under this category. Proposals are also part of the collateral materials mix; essentially, a proposal is a brochure tailored to a specific project.

The most important rule for creating a brochure is to keep it flexible and dynamic, capable of being changed as necessary. This allows you to tailor your brochure to a specific client and to keep your brochure current at all times. A permanently-bound booklet will be out of date in a year; but because of the investment, you will probably use it for three or four. A good idea is to use individual sheets that can be spiral-bound. It is advisable to use a few pictures—they should always be in color unless you use black-and-white images for an artistic expression. Professional photography is a must; otherwise, your brochure may look too cheap, which in turn can have a negative effect on your corporate image. To save money, minimize the use of color photographs, or print in color on-demand instead of pre-printing expensive four-color sheets.

Newsletters should be anywhere from two to six pages, and must be interesting! A newsletter containing "news to use" will get read, while a newsletter containing "pats on the back" won't. The main purpose of a newsletter is to promote name recognition and build a solid reputation of performance. A good newsletter will contain a combination of informative articles and promotional articles. Mail it consistently, a minimum of four times per year. Using desktop publishing and personal computers with mail-merge software, newsletters can be a very powerful marketing investment.

Proposal preparation is a communication form unto itself. Rules to remember: Answer all questions in the RFP, follow all directions, keep it short, and make it easy-to-read. State the problem, describe your solution in enough detail for understanding, but do not give away all the details that could get to a competitor. Describe the qualifications of your management team and outline the schedule. Explain your method of calculating the price, and leave a few items open to negotiation. Add a few descriptions of similar projects your firm has successfully completed to demonstrate your competence.

A slightly different version of this article, Organizing for Business Development, *originally appeared in the National Electrical Contractors Association* Marketing Advice & Customer Relations Report, *May 1993.*

Branching Out: Market Expansion Through Satellite Offices

Your firm is growing. With increased workload comes increased staffing requirements. More mouths to feed. More computers to purchase. Greater office space needs. But you are a growing firm, and growing pains are part of the equation.

The question, however, is whether you can sustain the volume of work you are performing. Can you continue to grow? There is a delicate balancing act between the workload requirements of your firm, the workload requirements of your competitors, and the workload being provided by your geographic target market.

Since the logistical concept of Just-In-Time (JIT) Delivery became prevalent in the service sector, most A/E/C firms have found themselves on somewhat of a rollercoaster ride. You are cruising along at an acceptable pace, with new business feeding the monster that is your workload requirement, and suddenly it hits: not just one, but several clients have large projects that they need delivered *yesterday*. A major spike in your workload.

Your immediate concern, of course, is how to deliver the product on time. Do you hire more staff? Do you use temporary help? Do you "feed the competition"? Depending upon how big the spike is, many firms employ two or all three options.

But gearing up to handle booked work is a tactical decision. Marketers need to think in strategic terms: how will we maintain our annual volume when we are through this spike? What steps should be taken now so we will have enough work in one year to feed this *workload monster*?

Any geographic area—no matter how fast it is growing—can only produce so much work for A/E/C firms. Small firms with minimal workload requirements can stay local. Mid-sized firms with larger workload requirements need to think more regional. In many cases, you can produce a higher volume of work over a greater geographic area from one office.

But in many other instances you will not be successful doing this. Technology allows us to perform work around the world from a computer and an Internet connection. Practicality interferes with that capability. Sometimes, you are just too far away to effectively deliver the product.

Satellite offices offer an attractive option for a number reasons. First, a new office in a new locality opens new markets. Second, a new office can generate work for both the minimal staff of the satellite office and the home office "workload monster," which continually devours projects and screams for more.

Depending upon the market segments you service, you may find that there are many—or few—prospects and clients willing to work with out-of-town firms. If you offer a unique service or operate within a unique market segment, you will be able to cover a large geographic area from one office. But if you offer a service that is not unique to a market that is not unique, why would non-local clients hire you? They can get the same thing from the firm down the street.

As unfortunate as it is, marketers in the architectural, engineering, and construction fields must accept that the services we provide are viewed as a commodity. Sure, we use fancy terms like "relationship marketing," but so does everyone else. Try as we may, sometimes we just can't effectively differentiate ourselves from the competition. So it comes down to who you know. And this can be a great marketing strategy in your home territory.

But as your firm grows and your workload requirements increase, you may have to look over a larger geographic radius to satisfy your sales goals. If you lack the interpersonal relationships—the network of contacts—you will be viewed as an "out-of-towner" trying to muscle your way into the local market. Of course, sometimes this can work to your advantage, if you can successfully position yourself as the *Out-of-Town Expert*. However, more often than not, the prospects you covet will feel more comfortable with a local firm.

So what is the way around this? Become the local firm.

When looking into market expansion through satellite offices, you have a number of options. First, you can employ a "cold start," whereby you open a new office from scratch. Most of these begin with a desk, a telephone, and a business developer who spends one or two days a week tending to the needs of this office, seeking to make new contacts and create sales leads and eventually bookings.

Or, you can strategically align with an existing firm. Perhaps you can bring something to the table that this firm lacks. Find a firm that matches your needs in a market you covet, and develop a strategic alliance or a permanent joint venture. Ideally, you can even sublease space in their office.

Finally, the most financially risky option: Purchase an existing firm. Maybe the makeup of the firm is similar to your firm, and allows you to expand your existing services to a new geographic market. Or, perhaps you make a strategic decision to purchase a firm that offers different services or serves a different market.

Before seriously thinking about a satellite office, you must first conduct a market analysis. If you are employing the "cold start" concept, you will want to focus on existing services and existing client types in new geographic areas. If you are an architectural firm specializing in commercial facilities, you should seek to provide architectural services to commercial clients in a new area. Just because there will be a booming K-12 market over the next decade doesn't mean you should be there.

You needn't hire a marketing consultant to perform this market analysis. You probably already have much of the information you will need at your disposal. To determine where you should be, you have to look at where you already are. A good first step is to review your sales over the past five years. From which industry segments have they come? Manufacturing? Schools? Churches? Bridges? If you are a niche firm, it should be quite obvious. If you are more of a generalist, you may need to do some work.

Based upon fees earned, rank your top three market segments, and the percentage of workload they account for annually. Are there any trends? Is one market segment growing and the others shrinking? Now, compare your bookings with national and regional industry trends. Information is readily available through the Internet, local business journals, and trade publications. Do these trends match your past performance?

When researching new areas for expansion, don't limit yourself. Just because you *think* you belong in an area doesn't necessarily mean you actually *should* be in that area. Develop some general criteria for this satellite office. If you have had success within 100 miles of your existing office, is there any reason to have a second office within this radius? Will you be staffing this office immediately, or will it be staffed part-time with people who work in the home office? If so, what is the maximum distance you will want people to be driving to reach the satellite office?

If you are looking to strategically align or purchase a firm, it could be one across town who services a different clientele.

How will the satellite office be managed? Will you hire a stranger to your firm who knows the locality, or reassign a manager within your firm who doesn't know the locality?

So where do you go for information? The book of lists and market demographic reports produced by most business journals are a good start. So are industry directories, which can be purchased from many vendors. The Internet provides a plethora of information for those who are patient. Listings of schools, hospitals, manufacturers, etc. can be found. Many organizations—both trade and professional—have online listings of membership; however, many of these online directories prohibit commercial use. Still, they can certainly give you a feel for the market and the opportunities.

In your research, you may find that to do business in a state, you must have an office in that state. Or to do business in a region, you must have an office in that region. Many state agencies throughout the country post A/E/C contract opportunities online. Whether you design highways or build state schools, this is another good way to get a feel for the market.

When employing the cold start, you must be patient. Remember, you don't win 'em all in your home market—where people already know you and your firm. If you open an office in a new geographic area, and know few people, it is going to take a lot longer. As it is, when you are known, project incubation can be anywhere from six months to over two years or more. With a new office in a new area, you must first establish name recognition and a network of contacts. Only then will you have a reasonable shot at getting projects—projects that will have that same six-month to two-year incubation.

Do not pull the plug if you have not been successful after the first year. At a minimum, you should commit to two years. If you are not seeing results at the end of the second year, evaluate whether you are receiving opportunities. If so, why haven't you been successful? Are your prices not competitive? Or have the projects simply not progressed beyond the planning stage?

Satellite offices provide an opportunity to expand into new markets and ship work to the home office to feed the workload monster. They are not without risk; however, this risk can be greatly minimized by performing a competent up-front market analysis.

A slightly different version of this article, Expand Your Market Through Satellite Offices, *originally appeared in the Society for Marketing Professional Services* Marketer, *December 1998.*

Does the Internet Herald the Death of Customer Service?

The Internet is an amazing tool. We use it to research prospects and competitors. We create Web sites to promote our companies. We read newspapers from far-off places, plan our vacations, and purchase products.

Unfortunately, while many of us have realized the potential of the Internet and use it regularly, there are others who relegate it to a lower rung on the corporate ladder. The result: incomplete information on the Web site or—even worse—lack of follow-through by those with Web site responsibilities.

I've recently experienced a rash of customer service gaffes. Here are a few:

I was interested in learning more about a real estate property for sale. I found an advertisement for the real estate agency handling the property—they were promoting their Web site as a source for information on local properties. Unfortunately, their Web site contained little useful information, and no information whatsoever for any specific properties. In fact, there was an apology on the home page and a promise to upgrade the site soon. In the interim, they provided an e-mail address for any property inquiries. I sent an e-mail explaining my interest to learn more about the property, and asked that they get in touch with me.

I never heard from them. Perhaps they were too busy cold calling prospects that they didn't have time to respond to us warm prospects. Interestingly, I inquired three times with another real estate firm before receiving a response regarding a different property. When they finally did respond to my e-mail(s), it was obvious that I was bothering them. They informed me that nothing would be happening with the property any time soon. End of story. Goodbye. No suggestion of alternative properties much less a suggestion that we get together to discuss my needs and their recommendation for fulfilling those needs.

So much for customer service.

In two other recent instances, I tried to contact both my local newspaper and cable provider. Because my concerns were only minor (a few missed newspaper deliveries, two channels with poor signals), I decided to rely on their customer service e-mail addresses—which they had been promoting—to share my comments. As it turned out, my concerns were apparently so minor that neither company felt the need to acknowledge my e-mail.

Finally—and this is my favorite—I decided to order a product from a company with which I was not familiar. I had spent a few hours on the Internet researching the product, then relied on the online buyers' guide of a reputable magazine. I placed my secure order online and awaited some sort of e-mail confirmation. None came, which is quite unusual—most online retailers have an automatic response system. So I revisited their Web site, found the e-mail address for order inquiries, and sent a note asking them to verify receipt of my order. Again, I did not receive a response.

At this point, I decided a little old-fashioned ingenuity was in order: I picked up the phone and called their 800 number which, of course, was out of service. I tried their local number and was greeted by a recording that said, "We're not in." Hmm... Well, after a little more digging I learned that the company was no longer in business! However, they hadn't bothered to inform their Webmaster and, as a result, were still accepting online orders!

How many times have you attempted to fill out and submit an online form, only to receive an error message that the form couldn't be processed? Or clicked on an e-mail hyperlink and sent a message only to receive a return e-mail informing you that the e-mail address is incorrect?

Unfortunately, these are only a few examples of poor customer service. In our rush to be online, we have lost site of the elements that made us successful to begin with. If you received a voice mail from an interested prospect, you would return the call, right? Most of us would be beside ourselves trying to return the call...our fingers would be dialing so fast they would be stumbling over one another! If someone walked up to you at a trade show and told you that they had an upcoming project and were interested in your firm, you wouldn't pretend they didn't exist, would you?

Recently, I received a call from a former coworker. She is a manager at a mid-sized engineering firm. One of her clients asked her to find an institutional architect with a national reputation. She contacted me for a recommendation. Two or three firms immediately came to mind. I knew they all had an Internet presence and gave her their URLs. While I was still on the telephone with her, she typed in the first Web site address. Unfortunately, she didn't have the proper plug-in required to view their home page. It wouldn't load on her computer! No option to pull up a less flashy site! For her—a warm prospect—to view this firm's information, she was required to go to another Web site and download a plug-in, then return to the initial Web site. Isn't this like not answering phone calls? Or keeping your office door locked at all times? Talk about making someone feel unwelcome!

Why should the rules be any different for Internet marketing and customer service?

My e-mail address (as well as phone and address) is listed on several corporate Web sites as a contact for more information. More often than not, e-mail I receive from these sites falls under the category of junk mail: someone wanting to sell me something. Occasionally, I receive a resume from a college student wanting a job. If they live or go to school locally, I'm happy to respond. If they are from another country, well, I have an "itchy" delete trigger finger! Other times I receive e-mail from overseas firms wanting to do the production of my drawings for some exceptionally low rate, equivalent to minimum wage in the United States.

In other words, there is a high probability that the e-mail I receive from my Web site is useless; however, there is also a possibility that it is not. To me, that makes it worthwhile to read every e-mail, regardless of the subject line.

The moral of this story? Unless you provide the same level of marketing responsiveness and customer service to your Internet prospects that you provide to your other prospects, it's probably time to "get offline!"

A slightly different version of this article, Does the Internet Herald the Death of Customer Service?, *originally appeared in the Society for Marketing Professional Services* Marketer, *April 2000.*

Is Your Web Site Giving Away Too Much Information?

Okay, so you've finally jumped on the bandwagon. You've developed a Web site. Good for you: welcome to cyberspace!

Can you do me a favor, though? Will you e-mail me your Internet address? See, chances are that you have unintentionally provided the world with a rather large peek into the confidential aspects of your business. And hey, if I'm your competitor, I thank you!

When developing your Web site, did you spend too much time focusing on the content that you think your prospects want to read, and not enough time thinking about how much information you are giving to your competitors? Like it or not, a rather large number of the hits your Web site receives are actually from competitors looking at your site for competitive information, leads, personnel, projects, and general design and content information.

Remember that everything on your Web site is open to the world, and thus your competition. I've seen Web sites that actually list client references. References! Instead of stating "We are pleased to provide this list of satisfied clients and encourage you to contact them," it would probably be more appropriate to state: "Dear Competitor, if you would like to steal my clients, here are their names and numbers."

Sound far-fetched? Ever get your hands on a competitor's brochure and think to yourself, "Gold Mine!"?

Yes, this is a fairly obvious faux paux. Most of us realize the pitfalls of listing our clients and their contact information. Yet we love to market our staff. "Our staff is our real strength." We've all used this cliché. Why? Because it is true! Our clients aren't purchasing a manufactured product. They are purchasing people.

We all work really hard on staff development. We recruit at colleges, then spend thousands upon thousands of dollars in training, both internal and external. Sometimes, we place advertisements in newspapers and trade journals, and are fortunate to have quality candidates apply for positions within our firm. Other times, we contact people we've worked with in the past, and ask them to consider employment at our companies. And yet other times we hire headhunters to do our dirty work.

But when the shoe is on the other foot and we lose a good employee—someone in whom we've invested countless hours and dollars—we aren't too happy. No manager is thrilled to learn that a headhunter or competitor has been contacting his or her employees.

The last thing we want to do is make it easy for our staff to be recruited. So what do we do? We list them on our Web site, along with their education, licenses, and project experience.

So again, if you happen to be my competitor, I'd appreciate it if you would e-mail me your Web address. We're looking for a few good people. You could save us time and money by allowing us to pre-screen candidates on your Web site.

When developing and revising your Web site, here's a good rule of thumb: if you don't want your competitors to see it, don't post it. Further, if you don't want to make life easy on the headhunters, don't post it.

Aside from the company information you want to avoid posting on the Internet, there is another major concern: client information.

If you have an existing Web site, you need to review any and all client and project information that you have posted. If your clients' names are listed, do you have their approval? If you have a project photograph, do you have the client's approval? How about the photographer's approval? (You may not own the electronic rights to the photograph.) If you have a project description—square footage, construction cost, overview, etc.—do you have your client's approval to list that information? And, if you have their approval, do you have it on paper? And signed?

In our rush to provide prospective clients with a plethora of information on our project experience, we tend to forget about our obligations to our clients and their confidentiality needs. If your client hasn't signed a release permitting you to use their name, project information, or project photographs, get it off your Web site. You could be unintentionally compromising confidential information and irreparably damaging your relationship with them.

And since you've provided your competitors with information on your clients, they're already knocking on your client's door!

The Internet provides a great way to get your message to the masses, to make it easy for your prospects to learn about your organization, and to showcase your talents. However, you can also damage your firm and your clients. Before you post anything on the Internet, think twice. And then think twice again.

A slightly different version of this article originally appeared in a two part series in PSMJ Best Practices*:* Is Your Web Site Giving Away Too Much Information?*, April 1999, and* Is Your Web Site Giving Away Your Staff?*, May 1999.*

A Few Tips On Creating A Web Presence

If I have to read one more article about the "vast, unlimited potential of the Internet," I'm going to vomit! But, you do have prospective clients out there, looking for you on the Internet. Mind you, some of them have never even heard of you, but they are out there.

So why should you be on the Internet? Have you ever heard of Coca-Cola? Have you ever consumed a Coca-Cola? I recently read that Coca-Cola is the most recognized brand in the world. Everyone knows about Coke. Every grocery store and convenience store on the planet sells Coke. So why do they advertise? Well, there are a number of reasons why companies advertise. Sometimes they advertise to educate (an advertisement for a new medication that will help alleviate the systems of Medical Condition X). Sometimes they advertise to inform (an advertisement from a well-known company introducing a new product). And many times they advertise to remind (drink Coca-Cola). The key to successful advertising is repeated exposure. Advertising needs to promote a consistent message that is seen often by the intended target audience.

So what does Coca-Cola have do to with your Web site? As it turns out, a heck of a lot! For your Web site to be effective, it not only needs to have people viewing it, but it needs to have these same people viewing it *often.* The first time they visit it, they may be educated (Pyramid Design Group provides architectural and construction solutions for people wanting pyramid-shaped homes). Or, perhaps they already know about Pyramid Design, and when they visit the site they will become informed (Pyramid Design was recently recognized by the American Institute of Architects). Think of your Web site as an advertisement that is running non-stop.

So now I, prospective client of Pyramid Design, know that they exist, and I know that they are an award-winning firm. I decide to visit Pyramid Design Group's Web site a few months later. What if nothing has changed? What if it is the same "commercial" that was "running" six months ago?

An effective Web site must be dynamic. Obviously, it won't be changing weekly—or perhaps not even monthly—but it should always be current. And, there should be an incentive for readers to return to the site. Information is the key. Keep me regularly informed, and I am more apt to return to your Web site. Again and again. If you don't change your site, I'll lose interest. If Coca-Cola needs to remind people that their product exists, Pyramid Design sure as heck needs keep their name in front of prospects and clients.

Here is another idea to generate interest in a Web site and build your corporate image: offer "news to use." Most small and mid-size businesses utilize their Web sites as merely nothing more than a digital brochure. Because of this, most industry Web sites look the same. However, if you create customized, educational content, your Web site will stand out from the crowd. Do you publish a newsletter? If so, does the editorial typically feature self-laudatory hyperbole or information of use to your clients and prospective clients? In the case of the latter, you may already have archives filled with educational content that is almost Web-ready. Don't hide it—share it!

Your Web site need not be "fancy." Sure, it should not be offensive to the eyes, but the emphasis should be on content, not design. Graphics should be kept to a minimum (if it takes too long to open a page, people will get bored and move on to another site). Maybe include a photograph of your office building, key staff members, and a few key projects. Be aware, however, that if you plan to feature completed projects on your Web site, you may need the permission of your client. Also, keep in mind that most visitors to your site will be sitting at their computer, cursing at the sluggish load time. Don't add to their frustration!

So how do you get on the 'Net? Or, how do you get a better presence on the 'Net? You have a couple of avenues. Ideally, you have the budget to hire a professional Web design firm. Remember, though, you do not want a site filled with the latest bells and whistles! Because you have no idea whether a visitor is running an early version of Netscape on a 56k modem or the latest version of Internet Explorer on a T-1 line, you need to design your site for the *lowest common denominator*.

Of course, if you are a small business, you'll want to keep your costs to a minimum. Here are two low-cost ideas:

(1) Do it Yourself. Before you shred this article because you think I've just destroyed my credibility, I want to let you in on another little secret: basic Web sites are easy. Truly. If I can do it, so can you! There are a number of freeware programs that can be downloaded from the Internet. Or, you can purchase a fairly inexpensive software program that can create Web sites far more fancy than you will ever need. Personally, I use the omnipresent Microsoft FrontPage, but there are many others. Most of these programs even have templates that can be customized, keeping the required work to a minimum. In addition, many ISPs (Internet Service Providers) have online applications that allow you to build a basic Web site with a few clicks of the mouse.

(2) Contact Your Local College or Technical School. Maybe there is a Web design student who would be willing to work with you at no charge or for a token amount. These students need to create a portfolio to help them gain employment when they graduate. They need you as much as you need them. Or, maybe you can find an instructor who is willing to take on your Web site as a class project. This would be great for you—each new class could be charged with revamping your Web site, allowing it to remain current and thus dynamic.

As far as hosting, you may already have space available, and not even know it. Internet Service Providers like American Online and Earthlink typically provide 5-6 MB of space for you to post your Web pages. Some ISPs have limitations on content—for example, no commercial use—so be sure to check their rules before you post your site. A typical web address would be http://members.aol.com/yourscreenname/.

When it comes to marketing your site, remember that your name is your brand. If someone is trying to find your site on the Internet, chances are that they may guess where to find you before doing a search. If your company name is Pyramid Design, the most obvious URL would be www.pyramiddesign.com. Yes, it does cost money to have your own domain name, but it doesn't cost much ($35-$70 for the first two years, depending upon where you register your site). If you want to see if your company name is available, go to www.networksolutions.com and search for it. If for some reason it isn't available, try adding a hyphen, or making other minor changes. If I were reserving a site in my name, I might try the following: www.scottbutcher.com, www.scott-butcher.com, or www.sbutcher.com. (In fact, www.scottbutcher.com was available, and that is the address of my author's Web site.)

To minimize costs, you can still take out your own domain name, and then "redirect" it to your personal AOL or Earthlink space, which you are already paying for as part of your Internet access/e-mail account. You can do this for free at www.mydomain.com. Through this site, you can register your unique domain name (www.pyramiddesign.com), and enable the redirection so that anyone who types in www.pyramiddesign.com will be automatically redirected to members.aol.com/yourscreenname/. The only cost involved is the $70 (or less) you will pay for your domain name, as well as your normal monthly ISP fee. Or, you could go to one of the many sites that will give you "free" space, which typically comes with a price: annoying advertisements that either appear throughout your site or "pop-up" every time a new page is loaded.

You need to get your Web site address in as many places you can. Submit your site to search engines. All you need to do is visit the search engine and look for the words "Add your URL" or "Submit a Site." It takes a whopping 30 seconds to add your site, though you may have to do it a few times over the course of several months. You can also go to www.autosubmit.com and utilize their free service to submit your site to twenty major search engines. Notify any trade or client organizations to which you belong that you are now online, including the local Chamber of Commerce. Search the Internet for architecture, engineering, professional services, facilities management, and construction directories, among others. Send an e-mail to their Webmaster asking that a link be added to your site. Include your URL in every collateral material that you send out.

Reciprocal Links. Contact your non-competing colleagues that have Web sites. Trade links. Encourage your visitors to visit your colleagues' Web sites, and have those sites encourage their visitors to visit your Web site. You never know where your next prospect will come from! Don't be afraid to promote your site. Do some Public Relations. Write a press release. Send it to industry publications, trade groups, e-zines, newspapers, and business journals.

Okay, so you are ready to make the jump to the World Wide Web. Here are a few more pointers to help create an interesting site.

Beware the Graphics Trap. We all like pretty graphics—they enhance the look and feel of a site. Animations can add a little pizzazz to the site, and make it more visually appealing. But, there is a downside: load time. If your page doesn't load within a few seconds, only the most devoted clients/prospective clients are going to stick around to see what's coming. Hey, face it—we are impatient. We want everything *now*. Or sooner. Don't annoy your visitors with long load times.

Beware of Fonts. So you have some really neat fonts on your hard drive? Cool. Don't use them on your Web site. Remember, anyone using your site is limited to the fonts they have available on *their* machine. This means that all the time and effort you spend to make your Web site look perfect are wasted if you are using anything other than standard Windows fonts, like Times New Roman and Arial. So, how come other sites have cool fonts? Simple—they are not really fonts. They are graphics. Graphics programs, like CorelDRAW—which I use—allow you to save fonts in a graphic format, like TIF or GIF or JPG. For instance, import a background photo into your graphics program, then type the text on top of it. Next, export the text and photo, together, as a JPG file. Which brings us to...

Know Your File Formats. Images should either be JPG or GIF for Internet viewing. These are the standards. While there are a variety of rules/situations for usage, I have a really simple set of rules: if it is a basic graphic or text, I use the GIF format; if it is complex—like a photo—I save the image as a JPG. As far as size, 72 dpi has become a standard for Internet viewing because of the reduced file size, but I do know a number of people who save their photos at 100 dpi because they feel it makes them crisper. Monitors can only display a limited resolution, which explains why photos look great on the screen but become very pixilated when printed.

Be Consistent. Consistency is a key to a successful Web site. As a viewer travels from page to page, they should always know that they are still on the same site. Avoid the temptation to make each page a different color or different background. On my Web site—www.scottbutcher.com—I use a consistent navigational scheme to make life easy for my visitors.

Avoid Frames. While Web Design Zealots would take issue with me on this point, it is best to avoid using frames. What is a frame? Well, think of those Web sites you have visited that had sections which didn't change as you went from page to page. Maybe a banner across the top. Maybe a navigational bar down the left side. These are frames. If you visit my Web site, you'll notice that as you scroll down the page, the navigational bar on the left disappears. That is because I'm only using a table, not a frame. Why should you avoid frames? A few reasons, but here are the most important: first, it is difficult to print. If you are in the "wrong" frame, you may print the wrong thing, like a header or navigational bar. A frame is sort of like a page unto itself, and you are viewing multiple pages at the same time. If you do not have the correct "page" selected, you will be disappointed when you view your printout. Second, frames are difficult to bookmark. You want people to visit your site time and again, right? So why make it difficult? Finally, some people are still using older browsers that do not support frames. Again, why make it difficult on your visitors? (That stated, some forms of redirection—e.g., stealth redirection—will pull your Web site into a transparent "master" frame.)

Be Wary of Color Choice. If you have a lot of text, you may want to consider a white or light gray background with black text. Reverse text (light color on a dark background) can be difficult to read after a while. Also, a red background with yellow text is downright offensive. Use it when you have only one word: WARNING! Or, CAUTION! Also, never use a dark background with dark text. Your site needs to be user-friendly, and thus easy to read.

Choose the Right Font. Huh? Didn't I just state that your options are limited? True, but here is a good rule of thumb: serif fonts (like Times New Roman) are easier to read than san-serif fonts (like this font, Arial). What does this mean to you? Any extremely long passages of text meant for online viewing should utilize Times New Roman. Many times, your visitors will want to print out your information and read it offline. Serif fonts make reading easier. That being stated, I've found that san-serif fonts work better if you have light text on a dark background.

Don't Make Your Pages Too Wide or Too Long. I typically design pages to be approximately 640 pixels wide. This is roughly a standard in the industry, give or take a few pixels. Why? It employs the "lowest common denominator" philosophy. No one wants to have to scroll across the screen because the text is disappearing off the right side. The 640-pixel standard takes 14" monitors into account. Most of us have larger monitors, which is why most web pages do not fill out our screen from right to left. Also, don't put a 5,000-word article on one page, unless you encourage readers to print the article and read it offline. If it is meant to be read online, break it into several pages, and add a link at the bottom of each page that reads, "next page."

Use META Tags. I'm going to wrap-up on a technical but extremely important topic: META tags. Whether you are developing the Web site yourself—or having someone develop it for you—you must be familiar with META tags. These are keywords embedded in the code. When you load a Web page, you do not actually see the tags; however, the tags are necessary for search engines to catalog your site. It also allows you to help customize how your Web site will appear on searches. For instance, suppose you are a small institutional design firm. Develop a list of key words that should come up when someone is doing an Internet search: architect, architecture, design, interior, programming, planning, institutional, educational, college, university, primary, secondary, private, K-12, health care, healthcare, medical, and so on.

Search engines will make note of these key words. Then, if I do a search on architect or medical or university, your site should be listed. (Of course, you may be entry number 2,534, which is why it is important to generate traffic yourself and not rely on search engines!)

If you are creating the site yourself, check the help menu to learn how to insert these tags. If someone else is doing the site for you, give him or her your keywords. If they say, "what is a META tag?" find someone else to create your site!

Well, there you have it. A few tidbits to make your site more user-friendly. I've designed a number of sites and, honestly, I'm not going to win any design awards. Note my apathy. Making a site easily read, understood, and navigated is far more important than winning a design award! Look at Yahoo! It was designed with content in mind, not aesthetics. Sure, your site should look good and even convey an image. But content is king.

At the very best, your Web site can generate sales. More likely, it will generate interest and thus create demand. At the very worst, it will still promote name recognition.

Lost Cost Public Relations

Probably every marketing article that you have read over the past few years has informed you that you are facing increased competition, as if you didn't already know. This article will be no different: Competition is fierce and your marketing budget is limited. So what's a business to do?

Focus on the public relations (PR) component of your overall marketing program, which should also include personal selling, advertising, research, and collateral material development.

In the past, "publicity" was the buzzword, and it referred to getting free press. While publicity is still an important component of any public relations program, the discipline has matured and encompasses much more.

Public relations need not be an expensive endeavor, though you will certainly encounter costs along the way. If you hire an agency to handle your public relations, you will most definitely encounter significant expenses. But since this article is entitled "Low Cost Public Relations," let us focus on the things that you can do through your in-house resources.

The most basic of any PR element is the news release, whereby you prepare a very short article on something newsworthy involving your company, and send it to the various media. If you are a small, local firm, you may decide to mail your news release only to the local newspaper(s). A more regional firm may elect to mail news releases to several newspapers within its geographic target market, regional business journals, and perhaps even a few select national trade and client publications.

When preparing your news release, here are some things to keep in mind:

• Make sure it is newsworthy; ask yourself if you would read it. Being awarded a project or hiring a senior level manager or estimator is newsworthy; hiring a secretary or pipe fitter is not.

• KISS — Keep It Succinct and Straightforward. Public relations practitioners use what is known as the "inverted pyramid," whereby the most important information is placed at the top of the release, the moderately important information in the middle, and the least important information at the end.

• Familiarize yourself with the recipient publications prior to preparing your releases. You will most likely find that most news releases being printed are only a sentence or two. Assume this is all the coverage that you will receive, so make sure your first sentence contains everything you want to appear. For example:

> *Dutch Country Mechanical, a fifty-person mechanical contractor serving the central Pennsylvania region, announces the appointment of Rocky Stallone to the position of Vice President.*

• Point out why this is important to the reader. Perhaps Dutch Country Mechanical is headquartered in the town where the release is being sent. Or recently completed a project in that area. Or Mr. Stallone went to college in or is a resident of that town. If you mail to local or regional periodicals, make sure you have a local connection, even if it means tailoring each news release.

• Write more than you think the periodical will print, but don't go overboard. Editors rely on news to fill their pages, and some days there is more news than other days. A news release printed today may only get ten words of coverage, while that same news release may get twenty words of coverage next week. It depends on how much space the editor needs to fill.

• Add your "commercial" to the end. Your final paragraph should give an overview of your firm. Again, you should keep your verbiage to a minimum, maybe only two or three sentences. Most likely, none of it will get printed. But every once in a while it will.

• Include a photograph. You are more likely to get coverage with a photograph.

• Contact the business editors to see if they would like news releases e-mailed. Simplify their job, and you will have a greater potential for coverage.

In some instances, you may want to notify the broadcast media (radio, television), but only if it is a special occasion, like a groundbreaking ceremony.

This leads us into special events…

The power of special events should not be underestimated—they can be a great public relations tool, if done effectively. Special events include seminars, open houses, and groundbreakings, to name a few.

A seminar involves hosting an event in which your clients and prospects come to learn. Seminars help position you and your firm as industry experts, and provide a valuable opportunity to give a "soft" sale of your firm to a captive audience. Perhaps you have the on-site facilities for such an event. Otherwise, you will have to rent space at a local conference center or hotel. To be successful, you have to be able to draw attendees, and the way to do this is to have topics of interest. You may find that you have the specialized expertise among your own staff to handle such a presentation. Maybe you will need to bring in an outside speaker. Sometimes they charge, sometimes they don't. If your speaker is a consultant and his or her target market is the people you are inviting, they may not charge you since they are getting free exposure. Another option is to invite some of your clients to serve on a panel.

Remember, you have to look at things from your clients' (and prospects') perspective: If you were in their shoes, would you want to attend? Some words of caution: First, make sure your speakers don't turn the seminar into a commercial for themselves or their company. Second, be sure you have quality presenters—you don't want to embarrass your firm in front of your clients.

The key is to create value. Your topic must be useful and *valuable* to the target audience; otherwise, attendance will be minimal. Make sure your company name and logo are on every handout, and don't forget to include your brochure and business card in the packet of materials.

Holding an open house is another effective way to create a captive audience of clients and prospective clients. Don't hold an open house just for the sake of holding an open house, though. Do you have an important anniversary this year? Did you recently move into new facilities? Is your office all decked out for the holidays? Maybe you can hold an open house as a business-after-hours event with your local chamber of commerce.

When planning the open house, here are some items to remember. First, are you going to have food and beverages (hint: the answer is *yes*)? Cold food or hot food? What kind of beverages—soda and punch, or something alcoholic? How many people are you going to invite, and of that list, how many can you realistically expect to attend? Maybe only ten or fifteen percent of the invitees will actually attend.

Consider having different activities to keep it interesting and keep your guests occupied, perhaps a demonstration or two or maybe even a strolling musician. Is your open house going to be for just business colleagues, or for their families, too? If it is the latter, you should consider something to keep the kids occupied, like a clown.

Next—and this may sound a little too obvious, but it isn't to everybody—don't forget to *clean* your facilities. Have everybody straighten their work areas. Touch up chipped paint, clip carpet strands, dust, vacuum, and don't forget the bathrooms. The idea is to impress your guests, not appall them!

A groundbreaking is another ideal public relations event, though here you will be sharing the spotlight (and hopefully not being relegated to an observer) with all the other stakeholders in the project—the client, community leaders, design professionals, contractors, etc. Working with the client and other important stakeholders, schedule a formal groundbreaking ceremony. Prepare invitations and invite the media (print and broadcast). Develop a press kit that includes background information on the project, the parties responsible for making it a reality, and a rendering or sketch of things to come. If possible, be sure to get your name and logo on all collateral material. Unfortunately, in many instances the client will do everything and you will, in fact, become the observer. This is why you need to be proactive and help your client plan the event, giving you an element of control.

Yet another low cost—but highly effective—public relations tool is community involvement. Participation on committees and boards of various nonprofit organizations enhances your image and thus your firm's image. If you give to the community, inevitably, the community will give back. Business leaders are often community leaders, and participation in the community's well-being will not only help to make the area a better place to live and work, but will also place you in contact with many high-level decision makers from corporations and institutions.

This is known as networking. It is a non-obtrusive way to develop business. Companies who give to the community—in terms of both time and money—develop a solid corporate image. You can greatly enhance your network of contacts, and eventually new opportunities will arise because you are in regular contact with the "right" people—people who will want to do business with you because of your commitment to the community.

Networking also involves participation in business and trade groups, from chambers of commerce to regional business alliances to construction organizations. You will get to know the business leaders and industry leaders. Sometimes, your competitors may actually make good teammates if you jointly pursue a project. Ever wonder how some firms seem to know everyone? And seem to "close" the sale before it even hits the streets? A good network of contacts goes a long way toward establishing rapport, enhancing relationships, developing opportunities, and closing sales.

There are countless ways to promote your firm without spending a lot of money. Participate in a trade show. Speak to a client organization. Publish an article in a magazine or newspaper that reaches your target market. Sponsor a hole at a business golf outing. Donate to your prospect's fundraiser. A public relations program enhances your corporate image, establishes your firm as an industry leader, and provides valuable contacts who may one day hire your firm.

A slightly different version of this article, Low Cost Public Relations, *originally appeared in* Pennsylvania Contractor, *November/December 1998.*

Open Houses as a Marketing Tool: A Case Study

When two sister companies in York, Pennsylvania reached their respective ten and fifteen year anniversaries, they decided a party was in order. NuTec Design Associates, Inc.—an architectural and interior design, structural and civil engineering firm—was celebrating ten years in existence, while JDB Engineering, Inc.—an electrical, HVAC, plumbing, and fire protection engineering firm—was celebrating fifteen. With one out of every three new businesses failing within their first five years in operation, both companies had much of which to be proud.

And since NuTec Design and JDB Engineering are located in the same building and under the direction of the same CEO, it made sense to hold their anniversary open house in tandem.

While a typical open house involves opening facilities for guests to tour and perhaps serving hors d'oeuvres and cocktails, both companies decided to make this open house a special one—not only to attract more guests, but also to make it memorable. So in March of the anniversary year, the centralized marketing department of the firms began to plan the event with two main objectives: 1) to have at least 100 guests; and 2) to keep expenses to a minimum.

By developing a timeline with defined milestones, the marketing department was able create a detailed, well-reasoned plan instead of a last minute scramble.

The first and most important decision to make was to determine when to hold the event. Both companies celebrated their official anniversaries in August, but with vacations and back-to-school events, August was seemingly not a desirable month. Because many societies do not meet during the summer months, the marketing department concluded June or July to be the optimal time frame for the event. But like August, July is a month when many people take vacation. In the end, the decision became fairly obvious: June. With the school year ending, most families don't have vacations planned. And with many community and trade organizations suspending programs during the months of June, July, and August, potential scheduling conflicts would be minimized. Plus, June is usually a comfortable month weather-wise. A date in mid-June was chosen.

Next, a day and time for the event needed to be selected. Friday, Saturday, and Sunday were not even considered. While many people are willing to forfeit one or two weeknights per week to attend work-related events, most are unwilling to give up their weekends. Additionally, Mondays are always an all-around bad day to schedule evening events of any kind. Thus, a Thursday evening was selected, with the thought process concluding that guests would be more likely to attend a "party" on a Thursday night than any other weeknight. In order to maximize attendance, a time of 5:00 p.m. was chosen, assuming that the majority of guests would stop at the open house on their way home from work. The planned time frame was 5:00 p.m. to 7:00 p.m., though 7:00 p.m. was only a time goal for internal purposes; it was not listed on the invitation in case any attendees wished to stay later.

After the date and time for the event were selected —and approved by management—the next step was to actually plan the event. Because the marketing department began planning the event several months in advance, they had the luxury of time to outline potential activities before preparing the invitation. They decided to create a series of stations for guests to visit. These stations served to not only highlight the capabilities of the firms, but also to provide entertainment for the guests. A list of potential stations—placed at strategic locations throughout the building—was developed, and in the end the following stations were selected:

Slide Show. Approximately 70 photos were chosen, some which featured NuTec Design projects, some which featured JDB Engineering projects, and some which featured projects designed by both firms. A narrative for the slide show was recorded with one of the staff members serving as the narrator. Background music was added to give the presentation a more professional feel. The slide show was set up in a small conference room. While the original intent was that guests would briefly stop in and view a few slides before they migrated to the next station, many guests actually sat and watched the entire presentation.

Civil Engineering/Regulatory Approval. A sample project timeline was plotted in color, highlighting the typical time frames one can expect for regulatory approvals. The intent of this station was not only to provide a source of information for the guests, but also to elicit questions about the process to be answered by the two civil engineers who were posted at this station. A healthy Q&A would help establish the firm as experts in the field and also provide the guests with valuable information. To take full advantage of the captive audience, several color renderings of civil/landscape projects were posted to show capabilities.

Computer Network. The manager of information systems was stationed outside the computer office to show off the Local Area Network, discuss the firms' computer capabilities, and discuss computers in general with the guests.

Electrical Testing/Power Quality Analysis. This station served as a demonstration, with computers being used to capture the waveforms of the office building. The process of acquiring and analyzing power quality data was discussed, and several guests asked questions regarding power quality problems they were experiencing in their facilities.

Interior Design. This was another interactive station encouraging questions from the visitors. The company's interior designer decorated the interior design station with samples of colors and materials that were popular at the time. Discussion not only centered on trends in corporate interior design, but also home design. Guests were able to discuss redecorating their homes and receive free advice from a nationally-certified interior designer.

Music Break. A classical guitarist was retained for two hours to provide background music for the open house. He was strategically positioned to maximize building acoustics. The marketing department contacted a local college to find a classical guitarist and hired a professor, who ended up being less expensive than guitarists advertising in the phone book.

Bridge Destruction. This station was intended to be a fun stop along the tour route. Since there are structural engineers on staff, their services were used to construct a small bridge made from balsa wood. Attendees were encouraged to make a guess as to how much weight the bridge could hold before collapsing, with the winner receiving a nice coffee-table book entitled "Structures: How Things Are Built." A time for "bridge destruction" was posted, and many attendees returned to the station to watch the fun.

Computer Modeling. The original intent of this station was merely to use one computer to display a 3-D model of a sample building. However, by the time the open house was held, the station had grown to include three monitors—one with the original 3-D model, one with a 3-D animation, and one showcasing the firm's detailed HVAC design.

Another important decision facing the marketing department related to food and beverages. Fortunately, the office building shared by NuTec Design and JDB Engineering had a large, open room usually used for training sessions and company meetings. This room provided a wonderful area not only for food and beverage to be served, but also for guests to congregate after touring the facility.

With the assumption that at least 100 guests would attend, the companies thought it essential to "do things right." With the exception of hiring the classical guitarist, there was minimal cost involved with all the stations, so "doing things right" in this case meant hiring a caterer for the event. An assortment of hot and cold foods was selected, in the belief that most of the guests would be having dinner later in the evening, but some would consider the hors d'oeuvres as their dinner. Additionally, the presence of a few hot food items enhanced the image of the open house and thus the image of the hosts. Having attended many events over the years, those involved with planning the open house concluded that no food or cold food only sends a message of thriftiness to the attendees, which in some people's mind is a negative.

Many caterers were considered and researched, and in the end a reasonably priced caterer with a good reputation was hired. The selected menu included a variety of vegetables and cheeses, as well as Danish meatballs and stuffed sausages.

After the food issue was tackled, the next issue involved which kind of beverages to serve. Again, the planners wondered if there would be a negative impression if only punch and soda were served. On the flip side were concerns regarding not only the costs associated with serving alcoholic beverages, but also the liability. In the end, a decision was made to serve beer and wine in addition to punch and soda. Like the majority of small and mid-sized businesses, NuTec Design and JDB Engineering strive to be good corporate citizens. Many times this involves the use of local vendors and local products, even though in some cases it might be slightly more expensive. So when it came time for wine and beer selection, the companies decided to use locally produced beverages. Further, they also decided to invite representatives from those companies to come to the open house and serve their product! Beer from two local microbreweries was chosen, as was wine from one local vineyard. An arrangement was made with the proprietor of the local vineyard, whereby he would provide a variety of his wines, and would take back any that weren't opened. He also attended the open house and served some of his wine, as did the proprietor of one of the local microbreweries. To maximize PR mileage from supporting local business, small signs were posted to inform guests not only who produced the wine and beer, but also that they were a local business.

On the subject of being a good corporate citizen, a "wall of fame" was created, filled with plaques received from charitable activities, from corporate giving to provision of volunteers. Again, this is a great PR tool that helps to establish an image of caring and professionalism.

The Mailing List

Just as important as planning the event is determining whom to invite. The marketing department debated how many people should be invited—the percentage of invitees that would actually attend was anybody's guess. Some statistics said only one in ten would attend. Others were both higher and lower. In the end, a decision was made that rather than setting a numeric goal, all current clients, important past clients, and important potential clients should be invited. A list of all individuals on the corporate database was printed and circulated to upper management to mark those who they felt should be invited. Additionally, a memo was sent to all staff members asking for names of people who they thought should be invited, just in case someone important was missed. Eventually, 575 people were selected to receive invitations. The marketing department decided to spend the money to print nice invitations, with each company having its own unique invitation in its respective company colors. Response cards and return envelopes were also printed, and a stamp was placed on each return envelope. The response card contained two lines for the names of attendees (as they would like their name to appear on a name tag), in case the invitee wished to bring a coworker with him or her.

The invitations were mailed approximately five weeks before the open house, and a follow-up mailer was sent two weeks prior to the event as a reminder to those who had not yet responded. The follow-up mailer listed information on the individual stations, the caterer, as well as the local breweries and winery.

Much to the surprise (and delight) of the planners, over two-hundred people responded that they would attend (37% positive response rate). In reality, over

180 invitees actually attended, far exceeding the expectations of NuTec Design and JDB Engineering. Also to the surprise of the planners was the presence of several prospects—individuals who had never worked with either firm, but were considered important potential clients.

Because the event was not only a celebration of the ten and fifteen year milestones but also a celebration of the people that made it possible, the managers thought it important to get all staff members involved with the event. Many people were assigned to the various stations around the building. Others directed guests to parking spaces, while still others served as greeters or worked at the registration table. Most of the upper managers were strategically positioned around the building to mingle with the guests. Additionally, all staff members were encouraged to invite family members to the open house, with the condition that they arrive after 6:30 p.m., based on the assumption that the majority of invitees would arrive between 5:30 p.m. and 6:00 p.m. on their way home from work. Family members were invited to come after this time, not only to keep the building from becoming too crowded, but also to finish off the food and beverages after the primary guests had completed their tour.

Was It Successful?

If you ask the managers of either company you will most likely get an emphatic "yes." Not only did attendance far exceed expectations, many compliments were received from attendees—both during and after the event—on the quality and professionalism of NuTec Design and JDB Engineering. The open house allowed the firms to showcase their abilities, to show off their staffs, and to create goodwill among their clients and prospects, all of which were initial goals in holding the open house.

But the event exceeded expectations in another way, as well. Three guests arrived with "gifts" of their own—gifts in the form of new projects. And these projects ended up being three of the largest projects the companies designed during the year!

Is An Open House Right For You?

Whether or not an open house is appropriate for your firm largely depends upon the reason for your open house. An open house can be a very effective marketing tool if:

- You are celebrating a business milestone (5 years, 10 years, 15 years, etc.)
- You have moved into a new facility
- You have renovated your facility
- You have purchased new equipment or expanded services
- You have many new staff members you would like to introduce

There are many other good reasons to hold an open house, as well. But you must also be sensible in determining whether or not to hold an open house. Ask yourself some questions, like:

- "Why would someone want to attend?"
- "Is it too soon since our last open house?"
- "Do we have the budget to 'do it right'?"
- "How many people can we realistically expect to attend?"

When choosing a date, don't forget to check the local calendar. Be certain the date of your event does not coincide with a chamber of commerce dinner or a society meeting. Don't just have an open house for the sake of having an open house...make it worthwhile for your guests to attend. Perhaps you can do this by having several informational stations and quality hors d'oeuvres and cocktails like NuTec Design and JDB Engineering did; perhaps you can arrange to have a "special guest" that people will come to see, or a special piece of equipment that will attract visitors. Assuming you have the budget and the time to plan an open house, the Go/No-Go decision on whether to hold it or not should boil down to one simple question: Would you come to your open house if you didn't work for the firm?

Does Your Corporate Image Need a Brand-Aid?

I recently attended a program on corporate image management. Having just read *The 22 Immutable Laws of Marketing* and *The 22 Immutable Laws of Branding*—plus, having just gone through a branding process with a nonprofit organization—I thought the topic was extremely timely.

Of course, the speaker was almost twenty minutes late. Then, she couldn't get her laptop computer to interface with the projector. Another ten minutes were wasted, and there was still no PowerPoint presentation. So much for image!

The content of the presentation was largely based on the aforementioned books, both co-written by Al Ries. If you have not read either of these books, you should. Both books are extremely quick reading, something of great value in our harried lives!

The speaker may have been an expert in branding—she may have been oozing with image management experience and credentials. But who cares? The "image expert" was late. The "image expert" was unprepared. Forget the credentials, what kind of image has been projected?

This is the essence of branding. Marketing is a battle of *perception.* Nothing more, nothing less. An example from *The 22 Immutable Laws of Marketing* clearly demonstrates this. Who was the first person to fly solo over the Atlantic Ocean? Charles Lindbergh. Who was the second person to fly solo over the Atlantic Ocean? Anyone? Bert Hinkler. How many people know this bit of forgotten trivia? Yet Bert Hinkler did it better. His flight time was quicker; his fuel efficiency was greater. In other words, his flight was of better *quality* than that of Charles Lindbergh. But does anyone really care?

Branding is perception. Lindbergh was first. End of story.

What is a brand? A brand is "a singular idea or concept that you own inside the mind of the prospect," according to *The 22 Immutable Laws of Branding*. Quick, name a safe car: Volvo. Name a cola: Coca-Cola. Name an overnight carrier: Fed Ex.

Is a Volvo really a safer automobile than a BMW? Does Coca-Cola really taste better than Pepsi-Cola?

Who cares?

When you go to a restaurant and want to order a cola, what do you ask for? Most of us say, "Bring me a Coke." Likewise, when you sneeze you typically ask for a Kleenex (not a tissue), and when you are cut you usually ask for a Band-Aid (not an adhesive bandage).

So what do Coke, Kleenex, and Band-Aid have to do with your firm? Actually, quite a lot. Whether you know it or not, your firm already has a brand. How would your clients describe you? Cheap? Expensive? Local firm? Educational facility specialist? Low quality?

If your clients consistently use the same word or phrase to describe your firm, then your brand has essentially already been established. And if your brand is already established, you had better hope that you actually want your company to be identified with that brand!

Believe it or not, branding is prevalent in the A/E/C industry. Sure, we never used to call it branding—we favored buzzwords like "positioning."

If I own a professional sports team, and I need a new stadium designed, who am I gonna call? HOK Sports—as if I had another option! HOK Sports is known for their design of major league stadiums. They have been branded.

Likewise, if I need a power plant, aren't I bound to contact Bechtel? Wouldn't I call Fluor Daniel if I needed a manufacturing facility or Heery International if I needed a program manager?

A brand is not a logo (e.g., a swoosh). A brand is not a tag line (e.g., "Just Do It"). But, if I want to play basketball like Michael Jordan, there is only one pair of sneakers I can purchase: Nike. If you want to take your children out for a burger, where are you going to take them? McDonalds.

The key to a successful brand is to have the prospect associate your firm—your product—with a seemingly generic word or phrase. The fact that we associate "McDonalds" with "kid-friendly burger joint" speaks to the power of a brand. Likewise, the fact that we associate "HOK Sports" with "stadium design."

When you think of branding, you must automatically think of the category that the brand occupies. Returning to the Lindbergh example: who was the third person to fly solo across the Atlantic Ocean? Come on—you know this one. Amelia Earhart. But do you associate her as the third person to fly solo across the Atlantic? Of course not; she was the *first female* to fly solo across the Atlantic. In other words, she created a *new category*. And, more importantly, she was the first person to occupy that category. If we associate Coca-Cola with "cola," what do we associate with Pepsi? Why does Bob Dole drink Pepsi? Why does Brittany Spears dance around in Pepsi commercials? Simple, Pepsi owns a concept not directly related to their *physical* product: Youth. If you are young—or if you want to stay young—you need to be a part of the Pepsi Generation. And that is a powerful brand.

Here is another example of category. If you want to take your family out for pizza, where do you go? Pizza Hut. So how did Domino's compete with Pizza Hut? They created a new category: pizza delivered to your home. Now, along comes Little Caesars, wanting to compete in the pizza home delivery market. But everyone already associated delivery with Domino's, so Little Caesars created a new category: Twice as much pizza ("Pizza, Pizza"). And how about Papa Johns? How did they choose to compete in the home delivery market? They created yet another category: Better tasting pizza ("Better Ingredients, Better Pizza").

In the A/E/C industry, there are many opportunities for branding. You can be "branded" as a specialist for a certain type of project. Maybe your firm owns this brand nationally—or maybe only regionally. I was recently speaking with a colleague who happens to be involved with a county fairgrounds complex. He mentioned their intent to build a new arena, and went on to tell me about this design firm that "does nothing but arenas for fairgrounds." Well, the firm—Bullock Smith & Partners—actually does work in markets beyond fairgrounds, but as we discussed, brands are all about perception. And this firm has actually completed projects for over 100 fairgrounds across the country. They own the brand, and thus they own the market. And when a fairgrounds needs a new arena, who do you think they call?

A/E/C firms can be branded by the type of service they offer: prospects associate "program management" with "Heery International." Likewise, they associate "cost consultant" with "Hanscomb."

Even a phrase like "abstract architecture" has for decades had a brand association in our industry: I. M. Pei.

Of course, A/E/C firms could also be branded as *the local firm* to call if you have a project. Over the years, I've actually encountered a number of these firms. It doesn't matter what type of building is required (e.g., hospital, school, office building, manufacturing plant), there is seemingly only one option—one design or construction firm that gets *all* the local work.

A brand over a limited geographic region can be just as powerful as a national or international brand.

If one of the keys to branding is category, another is focus. If you ask twenty clients to describe your firm in five words or less, and you get twenty different answers, you have a branding problem. Unless you are able to position your firm as *The Firm to Call* for a local project, the generalist strategy of trying to be all things to all people can only hurt your firm. And your image. And your brand. (And—even more importantly—your long-term profitability.)

The branding process is an attempt to control perception. Unfortunately, there is seemingly an overriding perception already in the minds of all our prospects: we are a commodity. Whether we are a design firm or a construction firm, most prospective clients view us as nothing more than a commodity; that is, we all look the same to them. We've harped on being the most quality-oriented firm or the most experienced firm or the most technically advanced firm. We have all told our prospects the exact same thing. We have homogenized the playing field. So how do clients differentiate us? Price.

And who really wants to be in that kind of market?

This is why brand development is critical to the success of not only our individual firms—but also to our industry as a whole.

One of the most important elements of a brand is known as the "brand promise." When clients hire a branded firm, they have an unspoken expectation of what they will get from that firm. A Volvo is an automobile. Their brand is "safety." And their brand promise? While they make no such claims in their advertising (imagine the liability), isn't there an expectation that someone driving a Volvo will survive a terrible accident?

As you develop—or refine—your brand, you must always keep the underlying brand promise in mind. Can you actually deliver? Sure, you can market your company in a way to control the prospect's perception; however, if they hire you based on the perception you created—and you don't deliver what the brand "promised,"—your credibility will be shot and you will have lost a client. And of course that client will tell other prospective clients and pretty soon the word will be out that your company creates false expectations that they can't back up with service. Just imagine the Rock & Roll Hall of Fame's reaction if I. M. Pei had designed a structure in the Colonial Revival style!

Remember the image consultant mentioned at the beginning of this article? The image consultant—lecturing on image management and branding—was twenty minutes late and unprepared. When she was asked to speak to the group, there was an underlying expectation—a brand promise—that she would *wow* the group with her experience and knowledge of image management. Guess who failed to deliver on their brand promise?

One final note on branding—the importance of consistency. Brands are not built over a period of months. They are built over years—decades, even. As you develop your corporate brand, you must have buy-in from everyone in the company, and you must commit to the brand for the long term. Any logo you create must reflect the brand. And tag line. And advertising, Web site, collateral materials, and PR program. But your brand goes even deeper than marketing. When branding a business or institution—as opposed to branding a product—the brand must become a way of life. The way your project managers interact with clients, the way your technical staff interacts with vendors, and even the way that the receptionist answers the telephone are all part of your brand.

A brand is the singular concept you own in the mind of your clients and prospects. Branding is an attempt to control perception so those clients and prospects associate your firm with a certain word or phrase. Brand promise is the underlying expectation a client has when they hire your firm. And above all, the need to develop or refine a consistent, focused brand should drive your entire marketing program.

Life in the Jungle: A Guerrilla Marketing Primer

"Marketing is war." This is not the first time you've read this phrase. In this competitive environment, you may have even found yourself using it. There was a time when you only had to compete with mechanical contractors. Then general contractors silently began acquiring mechanical contractors, infusing them with cash, a higher profile, and an enhanced marketing program. Now, in the deregulated electric utility environment, you find yourself competing with firms backed by deep-pocket, publicly owned companies. What's a firm to do?

Well, one thing is for sure: if you keep doing the same thing you've been doing, you will find yourself a casualty of war. A static, traditional marketing program is a recipe for failure; rather, you need to embrace the unconventional, to become the aggressor.

Webster's Dictionary defines "guerrilla" as "...being aggressive, radical, or unconventional." This is the concept behind guerrilla marketing, the strategy, and "Guerrilla Marketing," the landmark book by Jay Conrad Levinson, which has spawned a series of successful "Guerrilla" books.

So what is guerrilla marketing? According to Levinson, it is "Achieving conventional goals, such as profits and joy, with unconventional methods, such as investing energy instead of money."

Certainly, the idea of increased profits with decreased expenses is not new—it is a goal that successful business people strive toward on a daily basis. Note the presence of the word "successful." All too often we fall into the trap of doing what we have always done because it is "comfortable." But remember, marketing is war. The Civil War was fought with cannons, rifles, and bayonets. The Gulf War was fought with smart bombs. Times change. Do you?

Take, for instance, direct mail marketing. Are you making effective use of the medium? Perhaps you spend a lot of money on direct mailings, but really aren't doing anything noteworthy. If you have a newsletter, great. But everyone else has a newsletter. Do your direct mailers tout your projects, or do they give the prospect news they can use? Here's a quick test: pull out your last direct mailer, be it a newsletter, promotional piece, or letter. How many times does it mention your company name? Or use "we" or "I"? How many times does it mention your client or your prospect, either directly ("Company XYZ"), or generically ("you" or "your firm")? If your company name appears more than their company name, throw it away. You've wasted your time and money.

All too often, contractors and designers fall into the trap of telling their clients and prospects what they *think* those clients want to hear, not actually what they *really* want to hear. Face it, your industrial client really doesn't care that you just installed a new central plant for a hospital. A guerrilla marketer knows this.

I've seen many direct mailers from design and construction firms. Almost all have told me what they did for other firms, not what they will do for me. If you were a guerrilla marketer, you would have sent me a very targeted mailing, focused on a need I have. You would have given me an incentive to open the package, perhaps by using a plain white envelope with no return address (intriguing), or perhaps by using a light yellow envelope with something like "Ten Things You Need to Know About Indoor Air Quality" printed on it (attention getting). If I'm responsible for managing my company's facilities—and Sick Building Syndrome is a concern of mine—you better believe that I'm going to open your mailer. How would you know that? A guerrilla marketer would have done his or her research. Perhaps not necessarily on my firm, but on my industry. A guerrilla marketer stays abreast of trends, and develops strategies to capitalize on them. (It is not as hard as you think—if you read in the paper that a local school district is contemplating year-round school, it is safe to assume that they may need air conditioning installed in every classroom in the district.)

So I've opened your mailer. You have my attention. If you want to lose my attention, you will send me a boilerplate company brochure. Or a listing of clients for which you've replaced their antiquated HVAC systems. However, if you were a guerrilla marketer, you would use a black and red headline reading something to the effect of, "Act Within Ten Days and Receive Our Free Kit on Indoor Air Quality." Then, you would proceed to share with me some alarming statistics on reduced productivity due to Sick Building Syndrome, followed by some information on your kit and instructions on how to obtain it.

Any individual requesting the kit is now a qualified prospect! If you are a guerrilla marketer, you know that black with red highlights is very attention-getting; you realize that by asking for me to do something in the headline ("Act Within Ten Days...") you have increased the odds of a response.

Note that you haven't told me your qualifications to work with buildings with IAQ problems. Who cares? You are providing me with free information on Indoor Air Quality, thus positioning yourself as an expert in the field! You are being both unconventional and aggressive; thus, you are being a guerrilla marketer.

Yes, this is a very basic example of guerrilla marketing. But the key is to stop doing what you have always done, and not do what everyone else is doing. How many beer commercials have you seen in your lifetime? How many do you remember? Now, think of a frog. Does Budweiser come to mind? A bunch of frogs saying BUD-WEIS-ER is certainly unconventional. And memorable.

So how do you learn more about guerrilla marketing? Well, it is as simple as a trip to the local bookstore, or a few minutes of surfing the Web. Look in the marketing section of the bookstore for "Guerrilla Marketing" by Jay Conrad Levinson. There are number of additional "Guerrilla" books, including "Guerrilla Marketing Online," "Guerrilla Advertising," and "Guerrilla Selling," among others. Or, you can visit Guerrilla Marketing Online at www.gmarketing.com.

Remember, marketing is war, and if you keep using the same old tactics that you've been using, you will only be successful against those competitors using even older tactics. Lose the cluster bombing—go for the surgical strike.

A slightly different version of this article, Life in the Jungle, A Guerilla Marketing Primer, *originally appeared in* Pennsylvania Contractor, *September/October 1998.*

Promoting Name Recognition Through Direct Mail

Picture this scenario. Your firm, a regional electrical contractor, decides to offer a new service to correct power quality deficiencies in the commercial, institutional, and industrial markets. Since it is a new service, no one in your target market is aware that you offer the service. So you gather up all people within your firm involved with the marketing process, and hold a meeting to discuss promoting this new service. You then ask, "What is the most cost-effective way to get the word out to the right people?" Is it advertising? Public relations? Telemarketing? Direct Mail?

Chances are, direct mail may come up as the winner. Why? Direct mail is extremely targeted. It is also non-threatening to the prospect, because it does not involve a direct contact. Consider the options. First, advertising your new service. Where do you advertise to reach your target market? How can you be sure your advertisement is even being noticed? How much money will you have to spend to reach the proper audience?

If you serve several markets, like the educational, health care, commercial, and industrial, then just imagine how much money you would need to invest to place advertisements in the various available media to reach the proper audience.

Is public relations, such as publicity, a good option? If you mail a news release to the local/regional media, what guarantee do you have to expect any coverage? And if you are fortunate enough to receive positive coverage, how can you be assured that the proper audience is even receiving the message? Perhaps a small percentage will get the message, but the majority probably won't. Because of this, publicity should only be used as a supplement to your direct mail campaign, not as the entire campaign.

How about telemarketing? Is it wise to have a staff member call all prospects to introduce the service? To answer this question, place yourself in your prospects' position. Assume salespeople call daily to peddle one product over another. Would you want to receive yet another call? If you did take the time to talk with the salespeople, what would you say? "Send me some literature." Now if you are the salesperson, you send the literature and then follow-up with another call saying, "Did you receive the information I sent you?" Why take the time to make the first call when you can go right to the next step—mailing the literature?

There is a time and place for all of the aforementioned options, but consider starting with direct mail. The first, and most time-consuming step of the direct mail campaign is to conduct marketing research. The next step is to determine the content of the mailer, and develop an informative, good-looking piece. It is not until the third step of the campaign that you actually mail anything. Finally, the last step is to follow-up with the "warm" prospects who showed an immediate interest in your firm, as well as the "cool" prospects who didn't display initial interest.

Direct mail is a good, non-threatening method to make contact with a prospect. In addition, if you structure the direct mail campaign properly, you can actually elicit a response from the recipient.

Step 1: Market Research

Suppose you have decided to promote your message through direct mail. First and foremost, you must identify your targets. Who should receive your information? Which markets should you target? Once you have identified the markets (commercial market, industrial market, etc.), you must next identify the organizations (companies or institutions) to receive the mailer. Finally, once you have selected both the target markets and target organizations within those markets, you must then identify the proper individual(s) within each organization to receive your information. This can be a very time-consuming process, so consider doing it in phases.

Initially, start with your existing mailing list, if you have one. If you don't have a "formal" list, compile a listing of all your clients over the past five years. Add to that list the names of all the organizations that you have marketed over the same period of time.

Next, you need to "qualify" your list. Which organizations on your list would be most likely to have a need for your service? In our example, power quality correction is the service we seek to promote. Develop a list of criteria that the target organizations must meet. For power quality, your criteria might include that the organization be commercial, institutional, or industrial, but not residential. Next, you may want to place geographic restrictions on your targeted audience, or minimum company size standards, such as no less than 100 employees.

Once you have developed a basic outline of your ideal target organizations, match your existing mailing list to your outline. If for some reason your list is too small, consider changing the criteria to be less selective, like widening the geographic area. Next, confirm that you have the names of the proper individuals to contact. *Always* be sure to mail your information to an *individual*, not to *Whom It May Concern*. If your mailer is not personalized, it is all but guaranteed to get trashed.

After you edit and verify your existing mailing list, you may decide that your list is large enough, at least for the first phase of your direct mail campaign. If that is the case, you may proceed to Step 2.

More likely than not, though, you will want to expand upon your list, and this can become extremely time consuming. Take your outline criteria, and research where to find more names. That's right, research where to find your research! To simplify this, let us look at another example.

Staying with the power quality scenario, you have already determined your target market to be (1) commercial, industrial, or educational computer buildings, and; (2) located within a three-county radius. You have several options available for obtaining information on companies and institutions that meet both of these criteria. Your fist move should be to consult the local chamber of commerce in County *A*, County *B*, and County *C*. Inquire if they have a commercial and/or industrial directory available for purchase. Most will have one or both, and the cost usually ranges from no charge to thirty or forty dollars per directory. If the cost of obtaining the directories is formidable, purchase a few at a time, or visit the local library.

Another good item to check for is a list of the county's (region's, state's) largest employers. Usually the listing will also include brief information on each listed organization like Company *XYZ* employs 200 people, manufactures paper clips, is located at (address), and can be reached at (phone number).

Regional business journals can also be excellent sources of information. Many publish market research books, with various listings (e.g. 20 Largest Industrial Firms, 10 Largest Colleges). A trip to the library to look through local papers can also be beneficial.

In some cases, there may be a regional development authority which has compiled information for all counties in a certain geographic area. Also, look to the state(s) for information. You may be able to obtain a listing of state-run schools, or state-licensed hospitals.

Several companies have already compiled lists for any and every client type you can imagine, and would be more than happy to sell you their lists for a premium cost. These lists can be purchased (printed or on CD ROM) and matched to your outline criteria in general. For example, you may be able to buy a list of industrial firms in a certain area, but not a list of injection molding firms with over 200 employees. You can also hire a marketing research firm to develop a list that exactly meets your criteria. If you have absolutely no time to devote to marketing research (and do have the money), perhaps purchasing an existing list or hiring a marketing research firm will be your best option.

Once you have identified the appropriate organizations, the next step is to learn which individual within the organization is the appropriate contact. You may determine that more than one person should be contacted. For a college, the director of physical plant might be the proper contact. Perhaps you will want to contact the director of engineering at a hospital. Maybe the facilities manager is the correct contact for an industrial firm. Whichever the case, you must communicate with the organization to learn the person's name, correct spelling, and correct title. Also verify the mailing address.

One final comment on research. Don't forget to include on your list the third parties who might be in a position to recommend you to someone. For power quality, you might want to include utilities, general contractors, and engineers on your mailing list. Word-of-mouth is a great sales tool!

Now that your list is complete, it is time to concentrate on preparing your message.

Step 2: Developing the Mailer

What is your message? You must have an important message in order to create interest in your mailer. A boring letter will not create interest, and all your time and effort will be wasted. An exciting letter, on the other hand, can generate interest, and you should consider including some literature.

When embarking on a direct mail campaign, you must again place yourself in the intended recipient's shoes. If you are the facilities manager of an industrial firm, what information would be useful to you? Once you can answer that question, then you will have a good idea of how to structure the direct mail package.

In *Step 1*, much time was devoted to developing a targeted list of individuals to receive your mailer. In *Step 2*, you need to develop a targeted mailer. A targeted mailer is *not* a "generic" brochure with a form letter that says "Dear Mr. Doe, here is some information on our firm—please keep it on file." That approach is no different than knocking on their front door and pleading, "hire me!"

Instead of knocking on the front door, your goal should be to drop your packet through the mail slot in the back door, and then have the prospect invite you in! Power Quality is a specialty—a back door approach—for several reasons. First, not every firm offers a service to pinpoint and correct power quality problems. Second, it is an *ancillary* service, not part of a design or construction firm's "typical" duties. Thus, it is a back door approach. So tailor your packet toward promoting a specialty that you offer, like energy conservation, low voltage, intelligent buildings, green architecture, or some other niche.

Include a cover letter and, as mentioned previously, *personalize* it. It will have a much better chance of getting read than if you mail it to "Attn: Facilities Manager" or "Director, Physical Plant." The idea is to get your information in front of a prospect, so why shoot yourself in the foot by not personalizing your direct mail piece?

The letter should summarize the purpose for sending your information, such as: "Perhaps the greatest dilemma facing facilities managers of office buildings is the loss of productivity due to computer downtime." This could be a good introduction for the power quality service that you are marketing. You can also give facts and other pertinent information. You may even want to develop a guide or info-booklet discussing the niche. Everyone likes to get "something for nothing," so if you include a free booklet that will be *useful* to your prospect, he or she will be appreciative. And to show their appreciation, he or she will be happy to talk with you about your firm!

Remember, though, don't pat yourself on the back, and don't plead for their business in your direct mail package. The idea is to give the impression that *your firm is the expert.* That way, the prospect will come to you if they have a related need. And since you want them to come to you, some mechanism must be included in your direct mailer so that they have the initiative to contact you.

A very common method is to enclose a postage-paid post card for them to complete, not unlike the subscription cards that have fallen out of every magazine you've ever picked up to read. Give them a card with a box to check that says "Yes, I'm interested, please send me more information." Or "Yes, I'm interested, please call me." Provide adequate space for them to fill out their name and address, or place a mailing label—that already contains the information—on the post card. You may also want to consider adding a few check-off boxes to find out additional information or further promote your firm. An example of this is a line that states, "Which of the topics below are concerns of your organization? ____ Energy Conservation ____ Off-Peak Electricity ____ Intelligent Buildings." You may find that your prospect has multiple needs that you can fulfill.

Step 3: Mailing Your Information

You can handle the mass mailing yourself, with in-house staff, or utilize the services of an outside mailing house. If you are mailing a limited quantity, then there is no reason not to handle the mailing in-house. However, if you have a large quantity, you can take the mailers to a local mailing service and use their bulk rate stamp, which will save you money on postage. Call ahead to find out what their minimum quantity is for bulk rate. These services are useful because they will also perform the sorting, and most will also label and stuff envelopes if needed.

If you are not using a letter-size envelope, be selective in your choice. While a large white, blue, or black envelope will stand out, the standard manila is nothing less than boring, and your packet will end up on the bottom of your prospect's in-bin.

Step 4: Follow-up

Statistics tell us to expect a response rate of 5-10%. So if you mail 100 packets and get five to ten responses, your direct mail campaign has been successful. And any response you get becomes a qualified lead since the prospect is coming to you! Only after you get your foot in the door with the specialty should you worry about selling the prospect on your total package of services.

But what about the other ninety percent who didn't respond? Should you give up on them? Of course not. Even though they didn't respond, you now have a good excuse to call them. And there might be name recognition—which wasn't there previously—as a result of your direct mail piece. This brings us to another benefit of direct mail. It serves as a way to avoid cold calling. Even though only about 10% of your mailing list will respond to your mailer, the other 90% have most likely seen, if not read, your packet. Therefore, when you call they will be familiar with your company name. They may or may not recall how they heard about you. Either way, there is going to be some element of name recognition, though you will find that some of the prospects won't recall ever seeing your information.

Obviously, those individuals who respond to your mailer should be given priority for follow-up. After two weeks pass without hearing from the prospect, it is time to make a call. You should be aware that there is a limited window of time for follow-up. Wait at least two weeks before making contact to allow the prospect to receive the information, read it, complete the response card, and mail it back to you. However, if you go longer than a month without making the follow-up call, you have lost the advantage of having name recognition and your contact becomes a "cold call," which is what you are trying to avoid.

In summary, Direct Mail can be a valuable, cost-effective part of your business development program. For your Direct Mail campaign to be effective, though, it must meet several criteria. First, it must be targeted to the proper markets, organizations, and individuals. Next, the mailer itself must be both useful and informative. It must give the prospect a reason to want to talk with you, so promoting a specialty or niche is your best bet for success. You can mail it yourself or have a mailing service do it for you, but either way your envelope or flier must be attention-getting. Finally, follow-up with both the prospects who do respond and those who don't, but be sure not to let too much time pass before you make contact, otherwise you have lost the element of name recognition.

A slightly different version of this article, Promoting Specialty Business Through Direct Mail, *originally appeared in the National Electrical Contractors Association* Marketing Advice & Customer Relations Report, *April 1994.*

About the Author

Scott D. Butcher is the author of many articles on marketing as well as tourism and economic development pieces. He is a Certified Professional Services Marketer (CPSM) through the Society for Marketing Professional Services (SMPS), and has served as marketing director for NuTec Design Associates, Inc. (architects/engineers) and JDB Engineering, Inc. (engineers/consultants), both located in York, PA. He is also a principal with Butcher Consulting Group, LTD. Scott holds a Bachelor of Science in Marketing from the Pennsylvania State University and a Certificate in Professional Photography from the New York Institute of Photography. He is the author of *Simplified Architectural Photography* and editor/contributing writer of *Building Design, Construction, & Management: Tips from the Archives*. Scott can be e-mailed at scott@scottbutcher.com. Visit him on the Web at http://www.scottbutcher.com.

About Butcher Consulting Group

Butcher Consulting Group (BCG) is a diverse consulting practice providing competent, innovative, practical, and cost-effective solutions to the business and non-profit markets.

BCG offers a one-stop shop for business consulting, including:

- Start-up and management
- Collateral material development
- Marketing strategy and brand development
- Proposal writing
- Information systems management
- Web sites & new media
- Editorial & E-publishing

Visit BCG on the Web at http://www.butcherconsulting.net.

Printed in the United States
4725